SPONSORSHIP

STRATEGY

Practical Approaches to Powerful Sponsorships

KEN UNGAR

© 2020 SPORTS CAREER PRESS

Published & distributed by:
Sports Career Press
Indianapolis, Indiana

ISBN 978-1-7351731-7-7
First Edition
Printed in the United States of America

Book design and typesetting by Stewart A. Williams

CONTENTS

AUTHOR'S FOREWORD. .v

ACKNOWLEDGEMENTS vii

NOTICE. viii

INTRODUCTION ix

THE CORE ELEMENTS .1

What is Sponsorship?. .3

The Shared Target Audience 15

Property Potential Impact 27

Image Transfer: Sponsorship's Superpower. 45

What Makes a Good Sponsor Partner? 67

UNIQUE STRATEGIES 73

Business to Business. 75

Corporate Social Responsibility 84

The Pioneer Strategy 98

THE STRATEGIST'S TOOLBOX. 111

Strategy Within Contract Terms. 113

Technology Impacting Sponsorship Strategy. 126

Leverage: Turning Strategy into Success 136

Validating Strategy through Measurement. 148

Rethinking the Sponsor Summit Tool. 156

STRATEGIC THOUGHTS 161

ABOUT THE AUTHOR 167

ENDNOTES. 170

AUTHOR'S FOREWORD

I began work on this book in 2019. I finished *Sponsorship Strategy* in a different era completely.

On March 12, 2020, I began self-isolation at home necessitated by the COVID-19 global pandemic. In the ensuing days and weeks, the world changed for everyone. The consequent economic chaos ensnared many sectors but impacted the sponsorship industry harshly. At a time when humans cannot stand or sit within six feet of one another, sports and events, including the sponsorships around them, will find it hard to survive.

Part of my work-at-home regimen included finishing this book. During this time, I wondered whether a resource on sponsorship strategy would be relevant in a world that completely crushed the sponsorship industry. There are those who say the world will never be the same, and I agree with that outlook. However, I do not subscribe to the view that the changes in store for us will be all negative.

Without question, there will be challenges. We will

examine the sanitation and cleanliness of sports venues with new scrutiny. When the stranger next to us at a concert coughs, our guts will tighten. However, there also will be opportunities from this chaos. We are already seeing what technology can deliver to an audience at home and the value of entertaining content to people desperate for it.

I concluded that, like the world, sponsorships will have to change as well. We will not know *how* for quite some time. However, like in other challenging times in history, the successful doubled down on a smart strategy and executed it well. For this reason, I believe that a book like *Sponsorship Strategy* takes on a new level of importance to our industry. As management expert Robert Waterman once said, "a strategy is necessary because the future is unpredictable." For you, I hope *Sponsorship Strategy* is a valuable tool to face the unpredictable.

Ken Ungar
President
CHARGE, LLC

ACKNOWLEDGEMENTS

As is often the case in books of this type, many people generously offered their time and thinking to help the readers of *Sponsorship Strategy*. I gratefully acknowledge and thank many of my friends and colleagues. First, a big thank you to my colleagues at CHARGE, including Kyle Ginty, Ronda Hite, Sara Isom, Chris Myers, and Kyle Richert. Every day, these guys are out there helping clients traverse the choppy waters of sponsorship, so their insights were invaluable in writing this book.

I would also like to thank Elizabeth Naimbe, whose edits to this book were invaluable.

Over a career, a sponsorship professional meets colleagues in the industry who become as much teachers as friends. I have been blessed by learning from pros including Rod Davis, Mark Coughlin, Bill Long, CJ O'Donnell, and Paul Pfanner. I am indebted to the wisdom and experience of these friends.

NOTICE

I wrote this book because I love sponsorships and wanted to provide you with accurate and authoritative information to help you think through important issues as you build powerful sponsorships. But it is not a substitute for the advice and counsel of your lawyer, accountant, or other professional advisors. This book is sold with the understanding that I, as the author, and Sports Career Press, as the publisher, are not engaged in rendering legal, accounting, or other professional services. Laws vary from state to state, and if legal advice or other expert assistance is required, the services of a professional should be retained. Your sponsorship is your responsibility. I will provide you with the foundational knowledge of how business strategy works; only you can ensure your success. I do promise, however, that with dedication, perseverance, and a little imagination, you can build great sponsorship strategy.

INTRODUCTION

Anyone with capital can buy a sponsorship. If having enough money was the only prerequisite for success in sponsorship, then the position of Chief Marketing Officer would be the best job on Earth. However, the CMO has the highest rate of turnover in the C-suite.

Having worked in the sponsorship industry for over 20 years, I have seen spectacular successes and abject failures. The slim dividing line between success and failure is not related to having enough money. Sure, money helps. However, success in sponsorship, as in all forms of marketing, starts with the right strategy.

That strategy determines the *best* way to connect the dots between a customer's need and a purchase. Because the practical exercise of sponsorship strategy is complicated, mired with uncontrollable variables, and prone to consumer whims, experience often guides us as to what is "best."

My father often reminded me that "experience isn't the

best teacher; it's the only teacher." In marketing, my primary teacher has been the successes and failures of several decades in the sponsorship trenches. Sharing my experiences through *Sponsorship Strategy* helps me address a major challenge facing the $62 billion sponsorship industry: how sponsorship continues to earn support when competing for budget against so many other forms of marketing.

I started in sponsorship as a senior executive in the auto racing industry. Because motorsports is quite dependent on sponsorship support, I quickly learned how effective sponsorship works, how it compares to other marketing platforms, and why it delivers results for sponsors and properties. I also managed complex activation programs, protected my sponsors from ambush, and lost a sponsor or two. These experiences, both good and bad, led me to establish CHARGE, a sponsorship agency, in 2006. It was a place for me to help clients build powerful sponsorships, just as I had learned in the trenches of sponsorship marketing.

I wrote *Sponsorship Strategy* to help brands and properties use sponsorships more effectively. I also want to help those who dive into the sponsorship pool headfirst without checking if there is a tank of water below. "My CMO has negotiated many marketing deals, so he feels comfortable with a sponsorship agreement," said a colleague of mine who is a national advertising manager for a large, B2B products company. Most advertising executives feel the same way. If a marketing pro can negotiate multi-million-dollar media buys, a million-dollar sponsorship must be a snap, right? Probably not. Just as it takes experience to bring a great creative campaign to market, sponsorship relationships also require experience to capture opportunities and price assets.

When sponsorships lack proper strategy, they result in time and dollars wasted and potential minimized. Rather than celebrating the value that sponsorship can bring, poorly conceived sponsorships breed finger-pointing for the sponsorship's failure. Often, the sponsorship tool is blamed rather than the failure to use it appropriately. This hurts everyone in marketing.

However, as I will discuss in *Sponsorship Strategy*, it does not have to be that way. And, in fact, sponsorship can be the most effective tool in a marketer's toolbox, especially at a time when marketing channels are cluttered with the tweet of the day or the newest funny YouTube video. I want as many people as possible to know the best way to make sponsorships work. Doing so will make my job, as well as anyone practicing the art of sponsorship, so much easier with clients and colleagues.

So, why write an entire book on sponsorship strategy?

Most books and conferences on sponsorship today adopt a nuts-and-bolts approach. There are many great books on the subject. However, these "how-to" exercises are intended to help beginners hone their sponsorship selling skills and do not incorporate a sponsorship strategy.

I see the same tendency at sponsorship conferences. Attendees hear about a case study presented by the hottest brand at the NFL Fan Experience or a new way to leverage the latest technology for lead generation purposes. When getting together as professionals to talk about sponsorships, attention often turns to tactical concerns related to specific sponsorship deals. These discussions tend to be mechanistic and less useful to the sponsorship strategy process.

In outstanding marketing, the "front door" of the creative process is strategy, and the "next door" is implementation. Many times, marketers will bypass the front door and jump right into implementation. I see the same thing happen in sponsorship. As a result, tactics without strategy fall flat and fail to produce desired results.

That is why I wanted to leverage my experiences, the experiences of my CHARGE agency colleagues, my expert friends in the industry, as well as academics who work in this area to explore what strategies underlie sponsorship and serve as the foundation for outstanding programs.

In 2007, I had the same feeling about athlete marketing, an often misunderstood and underserved area of sports marketing. So, I wrote *Ahead of the Game* to fill that void. I hope this book will do the same for sponsorship strategy.

According to one researcher, sponsorship dates back thousands of years to ancient Greece, where the wealthy were taxed to support major competitions and public festivals and were honored by having their names engraved in marble slabs.[1] A business practice lasting 2,000 years must have some value, right?

Sponsorship continues to expand in volume and

importance. When I started in sponsorship over 20 years ago, the industry generated $13 billion per year globally.[2] Today, there are $62 billion of sponsorship in play.[3] By any economic definition, this makes sponsorship an area worthy of attention.

Seventy percent of sponsorships are found in the sports world.[4] So, for this reason, I will refer often to sports examples. However, there are significant sponsorships that can be found in a variety of industries and economic sectors. I will call out some of these prominent examples as well.

Because I am a practitioner with clients who must use sponsorship strategy, this book will be a practical guide. I will provide just enough theory to explain the strategic nuances of various approaches, blended with a healthy dose of real-world tips and application to create an impact in sports, music, festivals, non-profits, and everywhere else sponsorship is deployed.

The remainder of *Sponsorship Strategy* is divided into four sections. In Section 1, The Core Elements, I address the fundamentals of sponsorship strategy. I define sponsorship and key principals related to the shared target audience, the impact of properties on sponsorship and the importance of image transfer. The role of a "good" sponsor is also explored in this section.

In Section 2, Unique Strategies, I offer three approaches to best leverage sponsorships. I describe the important elements of B2B sponsorships, as they continue to play a key role in a sponsor's sales strategy. Corporate social responsibility is identified as a strategy of growing importance in the 21st century. I also discuss the impact of pioneer strategies that take first-mover advantage in a market, as well as their benefits and potential pitfalls.

Section 3, The Strategist's Toolbox, explains the interplay between key sponsorship tactics and their impact on strategy. I illustrate how contract terms must support sound strategy, how technology extends the reach of sponsorships, how leverage and activation build sponsorships, and how measurement must be used to validate strategy. Section 3 concludes with a review of the sponsorship summit tool, a much-neglected means to make strategies work better from a relationship perspective.

Finally, I conclude *Sponsorship Strategy* with key strategic thoughts. I reinforce several important concepts in this book, like authenticity, communicating the true purpose of sponsorships, and helping sponsorships live beyond the event venue. However, most importantly, I impart my core belief about sponsorships. Like the personal relationships we hold dear, sponsorship practitioners would be well served to think of this marketing technique like life. We seek friends with similar interests. We value authentic relationships with family and loved ones. We build these relationships through investments of time and energy. If we treated sponsorships like the personal relationships most important to us, we would know everything we need to find success with this powerful marketing platform.

SECTION 1

THE CORE ELEMENTS

CHAPTER 1

WHAT IS SPONSORSHIP?

A Definition

This book is about sponsorship strategy, so I want to begin by defining what I mean by "sponsorship." Definitions can often be foggy, especially for those of us who come from sports where business terms are used incorrectly. Take, for instance, the term "marketing." In some sports, especially professional auto racing, some say "marketing" really means "sales," which is not the meaning of marketing at all.

According to the American Marketing Association, marketing is "the activity, set of institutions, and processes for creating, communicating, delivering, and exchanging offerings that have value for customers, clients, partners, and society at large."[5] It is the first step in the process to connect a need to something that satisfies that need. Good marketing leads to product or service sales.

There are many ways to communicate a product or

service offering. Traditional advertisements and public relations campaigns were the primary channels that companies used to reach consumers in the pre-internet era. Today, there are a myriad of ways to reach consumers, many of them in the digital space. One agency, for example, estimated that now, marketers have more than 120 content delivery and marketing channels to manage – from LinkedIn groups to product receipts to mobile advertising. [6] However, for the purposes of this book, I will focus on one channel: sponsorship.

What is sponsorship?

According to the Marketing Accountability Standards Board definition, "sponsorship refers to a cash or in-kind fee paid by a sponsor to a property or entity (e.g., a sports, entertainment, or non-profit event or organization) in return for access to the leverageable marketing resources associated with that property/entity."[7]

Or more literally, the Merriam-Webster dictionary lists three definitions for the noun sponsorship[8]:

1. : one who presents a candidate for baptism or confirmation and undertakes responsibility for the person's religious education or spiritual welfare
2. : one who assumes responsibility for some other person or thing
3. : a person or an organization that pays for or plans and carries out a project or activity

The third entry could describe business sponsorships. However, all three entries have an important element in common: They speak to a *relationship* between one entity and another.

THE ESSENCE OF SPONSORSHIP IS THE RELATIONSHIP

Sponsorship works because of the association value between two parties. The sponsor, generally referred to as the "brand," brings money and marketing resources to the sponsorship relationship. The sponsee, generally referred to as the "property," has a desirable asset that the brand needs. Many times, in business, the customer-seller sales relationship is referred to as a "partnership." This definition may or may not be true as two parties do not always have aligned interests. Sometimes, the only interest is the exchange of money. However, sponsorship is truly a relationship in that there is mutual benefit and interaction that makes the relationship work.

We see sponsorships everywhere: the Olympics, the NFL, the English Premier League. Sponsorships are connected to the largest brands in the world: Coca-Cola, Honda, Malaysian oil giant Petronas. Properties and brands exchanging benefit in partnership. But what benefit do they enjoy?

From a macro perspective, the benefit is two-fold. If a sponsorship partnership is working, Coca-Cola, Honda, and Petronas are selling more products as a result. Additionally, their brands are perceived more favorably because of the association with elite properties like the Olympics. For the property, the primary benefit is cash: the sponsorship fee each brand pays for the right of association. However, each property also enjoys a brand benefit because global brands want to associate themselves with each property.

What Sponsorships are Not

In defining terms, I want to distinguish sponsorship from other marketing tools. First, sponsorship is not advertising. Advertising is "the placement of announcements and messages in time or space by business firms, nonprofit organizations, government agencies, and individuals who seek to inform and/or persuade members of a particular target market or audience regarding their products, services, organizations or ideas."[9] The crux of advertising is the *message*. The crux of sponsorship is the *leverageable relationship*.

At the risk of sounding obvious, this distinction is important for a few reasons. We see many agencies sell sponsorships on the backs of media deals. A seller of advertising will offer a media buyer a certain number of advertising units (i.e., 30-second commercial slots) and throw in a sponsorship opportunity as a bonus or value-add. During my auto racing career, I helped ABC/ESPN create such multi-dimensional packages. For auto racing events, I created event entitlement packages with sponsorship rights, signage, and other at-event elements. ABC/ESPN combined these terrestrial elements with TV entitlements and commercial ad units during race broadcasts. ABC/ESPN sales executives sold these combo packages to its existing roster of advertisers and their media buyers.

From a business perspective, there is nothing wrong with this practice. However, deals like this end up treating sponsorship as a media deal. This mutes the impact of sponsorship because the relationship is neglected. The media buyer, by definition, values the media buy rather than the sponsorship relationship.

Furthermore, when sponsorships are treated like advertising, a premium is placed on things like event signage and video boards. After all, visual impressions continue to be the stock-and-trade of the advertising industry. When this occurs, the sponsorship is measured only by media exposure of the signage. These may be important aspects of a sponsorship, and from a nuts-and-bolts perspective, media exposure is part of the valuation process. However, it fails to reflect the essential value of the relationship.

Second, sponsorship is also conflated with event marketing and experiential marketing. Event marketing is "the activity of designing or developing a themed activity, occasion, display, or exhibit (such as a sporting event, music festival, fair, or concert) to promote a product, cause, or organization."[10] Experiential marketing is "a marketing approach that directly engages consumers and invites and encourages them to participate in a branded experience."[11] Event marketing is about the event; experiential marketing is about the experience. Often, these items can be bought from the property separately. Thus, both may be – and usually are – part of sponsorships, but neither one alone

7

constitutes the relationship.

I've made these distinctions for two reasons. Only once sponsorship has been clearly defined can it be executed with laser-like precision. As I've discussed above, great sponsorship strategy is not the same as great advertising strategy. It is also not experiential marketing. This ensures that when it comes time to measure the effectiveness of sponsorship strategy, experiential marketing metrics are not exclusively used.

Why Sponsors Sponsor

Sponsorship is a pathway to achieve a business objective. So, why do sponsors choose this pathway? Sponsorship is a solution to a marketing problem. That problem may be related to sales, to brand and reputation, or some other vexing issue.

In a recent presentation given to a conference of sports marketers,[12] Bank of America CMO Meredith Verdone said her company engages in sponsorship for four reasons. In my opinion, her list could apply to virtually any sponsor:

DIFFERENTIATION FROM COMPETITORS

Differentiation is critical in brand marketing. Generally, a brand must prove to the consumer that its product or services are superior to or distinct from its competitors for some unassailable reason. Most times, this differentiation originates from the brand. Advertising or social media, for example, come from the brand's marketing team. When a brand brags about its own product, its credibility is always suspect. However, third-party validation usually provides the most effective means of differentiation: "Don't take my word for it. I'm different or better because an independent, third party says so."

Sponsorship serves as this third-party validation offering competitive differentiation. Especially in the case where a sponsorship is exclusive between a property and a brand, there can only be one sponsor in a category for a property. Bank of America is the hometown bank of the Carolina Panthers. Period. End of story. This has been a very effective strategy to differentiate itself from every other financial competitor in the Charlotte market.

In hyper-competitive markets, I have observed a gold-rush to differentiate by taking available categories. At sports events, beer and carbonated soft drinks are examples of this level of competition. Another example of hyper-competition comes from the healthcare category. Since the 2012 Affordable Care Act, which turned the heat up on healthcare industry competition, healthcare systems fiercely vie to be the official healthcare provider of their local NFL, NBA, or MLB team.

COMMUNITY

Properties and their audiences live in communities. A sponsorship, if planned and managed correctly (which I will discuss below), provides the entrée for a sponsor to show its commitment to a community and participate in some meaningful way. It offers a visible opportunity to interact within an audience's community that other marketing channels cannot provide.

I see this manifest in markets with large, Fortune 500 headquarter offices. For example, US Bank and Target Stores are well-known companies with high brand awareness. They do not necessarily need to engage in high-profile sponsorship opportunities. However, US Bank chose to align with the Minnesota Vikings' stadium, while Target lent its prestigious name to the Minnesota Twins' ballpark. In both cases, these Minneapolis-based companies wanted to demonstrate support for the community where their employees live and work. What could be a more meaningful way to support the community than to be a visible booster for the hometown team?

EMPLOYEES

Nearly every company has employees. When these employees are not working, they attend sporting events, support the arts, or engage in volunteer activity. They wear team jerseys, play fantasy sports, run 5k races to support breast cancer research, and take their kids to the children's museum. Employees are members of an audience for a sponsorable property. Like other audience members, they care passionately about sports, music, and the arts.

Sponsorships offer brands the opportunity to connect with employees outside work about things their employees care about. If employees love auto racing, sponsoring a racing event creates an opportunity to foster positive morale.

It adds a feel-good opportunity attached to an event their company is visibly supporting. However, this is different from a company holiday party or summer picnic, which has no visible public sanction.

In some cases, companies include their employees' families in sponsored events. Providing such a benefit, from an employee relations perspective, often creates positive and organic opportunities to demonstrate commitment to employee lives and families.

Finally, employees care deeply about causes close to their hearts. When their company demonstrates a tangible commitment to the same cause (i.e., tangible in the sense that the employer donates in support), the employee takes note of the special nature of their place of work. This is increasingly common because corporate social responsibility co-exists very nicely with employee cause commitments.

CLIENT EXPERIENCES

At a time when a client meal or round of golf just will not cut it, sponsorships provide brands with the chance to better connect with a client. I will discuss the issue of B2B relationships in the sponsorship context later in this book. However, I should note here that the creation of client experiences serves as a significant motivation to forge sponsorship relationships.

Some brands choose to invite their clients or prospects to any sponsored event – whether the brand sponsors the event or not. However, sponsorship often gives sponsors the opportunity to create exclusive entertainment options. In the chapter on B2B relationships, I will discuss how sponsorships can create unforgettable or unique experiences that forge an indelible connection between the sponsor and the client. Access to an athlete in the locker room, a hot lap in an Acura NSX at a sports car race, or a backstage pass at the dream concert are a few examples of client experiences built into sponsorships.

In sum, sponsors are diversely motivated to create relationships with properties. It provides a level of engagement and authenticity that other marketing channels simply do not. Finally, I should note that it is emotionally powerful for a property to endorse a sponsor. Marketers are always looking to forge emotional connections through their work, and sponsorship helps do that in a very influential way.[13]

The Sponsorship Formula

During my marketing career, I have had the opportunity to work with many clients who possess engineering backgrounds. With academic and professional rituals steeped in physics, chemistry, math, and other scientific disciplines, these clients constantly question which laws of science and nature govern marketing. I've yet to find a great answer for this question. If I could, I am sure that I could pick successful commercials, create viral social media campaigns, and forecast consumer behavior with pinpoint accuracy. While marketing is much more analytical than it was 20 years ago (thanks technology!), it is still not possible to use the formulaic approach one would apply to principles of erecting a skyscraper or building a car engine.

However, these engineering friends and clients have taught me that formulas simply describe a list of ingredients and the process of successfully combining them. For this reason, I have developed a formula for creating powerful sponsorship relationships. Although this formula is still relatively qualitative, it provides a useful framework for sponsorship success.

In order to maximize sponsorship benefit, sponsorship elements must be combined as follows:

(SHARED TARGET AUDIENCE + PROPERTY POTENTIAL IMPACT) x IMAGE TRANSFER = SPONSORSHIP BENEFIT

A "Shared Target Audience" refers to the customers that the brand and the property have in common. Commonly, the audience is defined in demographic and psychographic terms: who they are and what they believe in.

"Property Potential Impact" refers to property characteristics from a marketing perspective. These are the elements that make the property attractive (or not).

"Image Transfer" refers to the positive brand attributes of the property that benefit the brand as a result of the sponsorship partnership or association. It is the delicious chewy center of a Tootsie Roll pop.

The formula's first two elements, audience and property,

are factual, empirical, and measurable from the brand's side. They either have a shared target audience or they do not. No amount of finesse will help if the brand and the property do not share a target audience; such a sponsorship would be under-optimized. The same is true of the property. The property is either right for the sponsorship relationship or it is not. While the property characteristics can be managed from the property side, they cannot be changed directly by the brand.

The sponsorship starts with the additive benefit of the target audience and the property's potential impact. But the real magic happens in the process of image transfer. In military terms, this is what a general would call a force multiplier. It gives the sponsor the ability to achieve greater benefit with it than without it. Many strategic recommendations depend on sponsors aggressively managing image transfer, with properties making that possible by coordinating rights and implementation. But, again, the responsibility here rests with the brand to maximize sponsorship benefits.

When this formula is optimized, the sponsor enjoys a benefit that only a well-crafted and well-implemented sponsorship can provide. In the next several chapters, I will explore the components of this strategy formula and explain how using it yields more powerful sponsorships.

CHAPTER 2

THE SHARED TARGET AUDIENCE

General Considerations

One of my favorite lessons in business is that "order matters." If you have a list, the order of the items matters. It can be ranked in level of importance, alphabetically, or by age. However, the order of the list should denote something of importance to the reader.

Here, I have chosen to begin with the shared target audience because it is the most important foundational element of the sponsorship. If either the brand or the property gets it wrong, a sponsorship cannot succeed. They both must speak to the same target audience. When a shared audience is identified, there is a much higher probability of marketing success.

Why? The short answer is that, for the sponsor and property to work together effectively, there must be a community of shared interest.

Every property has an audience, and successful

properties are perceived positively. The audience appreciates some aspect of the property and is motivated to support
it with attendance and money. For example, one author in
Bleacher Report described sports properties with great audiences in this way[14]:

> These are not bandwagon fans, but rather, fans
> baptized into a religion at birth. The home stadium
> is the church and the team logo is their symbol of
> faith. These are season-ticket holders who skip wed-
> dings for games and arrange to be buried in coffins
> with their team's logo on them.

And it is estimated that these fans spend well over $100
per person to attend their favorite games.[15]

Similarly, every brand has customers. As is the case with
the property's audience, customers appreciate the brand at
an economic level, an emotional level, or both. Brands with
super fans like Disney, Harley-Davidson, and Apple have
certainly engaged their audiences on an emotional level.

When the property and the brand bond via a sponsorship, there is the expectation that their audiences align. It
is like the parties I used to attend in college. Every Friday
night, I would survey my roommates to determine (1) if
there were parties that weekend, (2) who was throwing
that party, and (3) whether I could attend. A major part of
these discussions entailed *who* was going to be at that party.
When my friends and I shared few-to-no interests with the

other partygoers, we avoided the party knowing that there would be little chance of enjoying it.

Brands go through the same process of picking which "party" to attend. A party with people who have similar interests will be a success. But a party with people who do not have a lot in common will feel like a waste of time.

To extend this party metaphor a little further, and apply it to business, the line between success and failure becomes clear. At a party with guests whose interests align, I will meet two kinds of people: people I know and people I do not know. The people I know are akin to a business's existing customers. We already agree that our interests align, so conversation is effortless and enjoyable. We share all kinds of information back and forth. The result of our exchange may deepen our relationship. For a business, this exercise increases brand loyalty.

The people I do not know are like new customers. As is the case with the people I already know, we have a set of mutual interests. Having something in common from the start is the ice breaker. It provides an opportunity for us to have a meaningful conversation with someone we can (sort of) trust because we share the same interests. By the end of the party, we may exchange emails or phone numbers to stay in touch. Either way, we both feel we have made a new friend. For a business, this process is known as lead generation and customer acquisition – neither of which could have happened without a mutual interest.

The process of analyzing audiences for a sponsorship

is a lot more technical than how I chose parties in college. However, at its roots, the objectives are the same. From a strategy perspective, it is important to understand the process of customer or audience identification. For purposes of this book, I assume that many brands have sufficient internal resources to really understand their customers. This type of market research is expensive and often customized, depending on the customer base and the product or service offered. Big data, as I'll discuss in a later chapter, has made audience analysis even more intensive. For this reason, many brands have a keen understanding of exactly who their customers are and the interests they have.

However, I have seen properties struggle a bit more than brands with audience identification because they usually have fewer resources to dedicate to these analytics. Frankly, given the capital constraints and operational issues that plague most properties, it can be a miracle when any resources at all are dedicated to market research. As such, many of the tactical suggestions regarding audience identification will be directed at readers who work for properties.

From a marketing perspective, there are entire books on how to understand a customer's distinctive traits, so I will not discuss them here. But the premise is the better you know your customers, the better you can connect with them.

Instead, the goal here is to use this Venn diagram to understand finite areas of overlap. This overlap between the brand's product/service audience and the property's audience is the core of the "shared target audience" component of

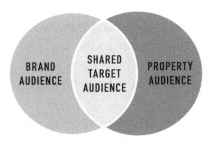

FIGURE 1 AUDIENCE OVERLAP

the sponsorship strategy formula. In order to understand the audience issue better, I will break it down.

In my college days, understanding a party was very anecdotal. I had no idea the exact background of each partygoer. I just made assumptions based on how a 19-year-old thinks of his peers. In business, the study of a customer audience is far more analytical. In order to best identify the shared target audience, you will want as much data about the audience as possible.

Data is gathered in a variety of ways. Attendees can be surveyed before the event, after the event, or at both points. Focus groups can be used to gather more qualitative information about the audience. Additionally, the proliferation of technology tools, especially those related to social media platforms, provides a rich trove of audience data if the property has digital and social media resources.

This wealth of digital data then needs to be sifted and examined in order to make sense of it, especially to identify customers, audiences, and apply it to a sponsorship strategy. This data is sifted in two ways. First, the data is segmented. Then, the data is combined into niche audience descriptions to make sense of the segments.

Audience Segmentation

A marketer will segment audiences in order to identify the best targets for sales and marketing programs. Although there are myriad of ways to segment customers, I have found four to be particularly helpful: demographic, psychographic, geographic, and behavioral.

Demographics are the statistical characteristics of a population segment, most often described with the following categories[16]:

- Age
- Gender
- Race
- Marital status
- Number of children (if any)
- Occupation
- Annual income
- Education level
- Living status (homeowner or renter)

Demographic characteristics are generally stable. I will always be a certain race, nationality, generational cohort, and my gender and occupation are unlikely to change. Some demographic data points have more relevance to marketers than others. A seller of hearing aids will probably be focused on an older audience, while a brand offering men's deodorant will focus on the male gender.

Psychographics "is a qualitative methodology used to describe consumers on psychological attributes"[17] . . . including "personality, values, opinions, attitudes, interests, and lifestyles."[18] Examples of psychographic descriptors might be people who enjoy camping, science fiction fans, or attendees of youth sports events.

Geographic segmentation data relates to where individuals live or work. It is a descriptor derived from the territory they consider home. Depending on the degree of specificity required, geographic segments can include countries, states/provinces, cities/towns, counties, or even zip codes.

Behavioral segmentation involves dividing the audience into groups based on their buying behavior.[19] This level of segmentation helps businesses understand how their customers buy in order to fuel sales. For example, consumers may purchase in relation to special occasions (like a holiday or birthday), to usage-orientation (whether users are heavy or light buyers of a product), to loyalty-orientation (the degree to which users are loyal to a certain product or brand) and to benefits sought (whether customers look for benefits such as low cost).[20]

Customer Personas

If the property hosts large events, there could be tens of thousands of customers walking through the gates. Thus, it is simply not practical to examine each customer individually. Rather, the art of audience analysis is the way audience members can be segmented, which means grouping customers by common traits. However, segmenting may or may not be helpful to a business wanting to solicit a certain type of customer.

For example, all 22-year-olds are not created equally. They have a variety of interests and motivations. So, using only the demographic segment of age is not entirely meaningful to a business on the prowl for new revenue opportunities. There needs to be another level of description.

This additional level of description is often referred to as a "customer persona." It is a niche combination of segments used to create easily understood descriptions of a consumer audience.

As an example, let us start with the age demographic and build several customer personas around age. Gen Z is growing in importance to many sponsors, because its oldest members have now joined the workforce, so I will use that generation as an exemplar. Gen Z members were born between 1995 and 2010. Generally, they share a few things in common:

- They are "digital natives," never knowing a world without the internet or smartphones.
- They are racially and ethnically diverse and will be the last generation that is majority Caucasian.
- They are entrepreneurial, inspired by how simple it is to start companies in the shared economy, like Lyft or Venmo.

- They demand the ability to personalize because technology has made customization possible in all aspects of their lives, including music and photo/video sharing.

Beyond those shared characteristics, different properties may look to service a variety of customer personas. An esports league may have a customer persona it calls "Hardcore Gamer." It characterizes these Gen Z members as:
- Predominantly male
- Plays video games for an average of two hours per day
- Consumes energy drinks and highly caffeinated beverages at a rate higher than the general population
- Enjoys salty snack foods
- Listens to music and creates playlists for friends
- Connects with friends every day via smartphone or online game.

An auto racing series may have a persona called "High-Tech Outdoor Enthusiast," which it describes as:
- Slightly more male than female
- Must own the latest technology or gadget; is generally the first adopter of computers, smartphones, or apps
- Enjoys at least three hours of auto racing content per week
- Loves to camp or hike with family and friends
- Interested in environmental sustainability

Both the Hardcore Gamer and High-Tech Outdoor Enthusiast customer personas help a prospective sponsor understand if it shares a target audience with a property. Even when a large number of customer personas is identified within a larger audience, each persona brings the parties closer to the same potential customers.

Practical Considerations

There are a variety of practical considerations as brands and properties consider the first ingredient of the sponsorship benefit formula. To understand the shared target audience dynamic, I recommend the following steps to ensure that overlap in the audience Venn diagram is as substantial as possible.

SOURCE DATA

During the courtship between a brand and a property, I encourage liberal sharing of audience data. While some data may be considered secret or proprietary, collaboration at this stage promotes the discovery of unique insights about a property's audience. Some properties may be concerned that too much information (or bad information) might scare off a prospect. But as with anything else in business, there are pros and cons to sharing data. Certainly, the property wants to protect its confidential audience information. Additionally, the property may be concerned that a potential sponsor will find contrary audience information later in the relationship. However, I argue that these issues should be sorted out before "marriage." The alternative is a messy divorce if a sponsorship relationship does not yield good ROI, which is many times worse for a property's reputation.

Shared information can include attendee surveys, attendee focus groups, and other direct source data. Similarly, various research agencies have developed important data sources that indicate how the audience is segmented. For example, a property can provide a brand with information about current buying patterns in the sponsor's product line. Information that the property's audience is three times more likely than the general population to buy the brand's product is important audience data. Additionally, if a property can show that a large proportion of its audience will be in the market to buy the sponsor's product in the next six months, the prospects for a good relationship increase substantially.

Many good sponsorship sellers include this information in a presentation deck. However, brand buyers should not hesitate to ask sellers for additional data. Doing so demonstrates the seller's willingness to go above-and-beyond.

GENERATIONAL DATA

Notwithstanding my discussion above regarding the isolated nature of looking only at the age demographic, examining audiences generationally offers important information about a property's audience. While age is just a single data point, the values and shared experiences of each generation offer more consumer insights than mere date of birth.

Of course, these generational insights offer more possibilities than simply understanding if a property and brand share the same audience. They help properties create generation-specific entertainment opportunities (i.e., certain music or technology amenities like Wi-Fi) or programs considered valuable by a certain age cohort (like sustainability or corporate social responsibility).

Actual Audiences vs Aspirational Audiences

I have seen confusion caused by conflating today's actual audience with the audience a property aspires to have in the future. For instance, in the US, the average age of fans in many US-based sports continues to increase. To reverse the aging of their fan bases, these sports are adapting their products for younger generations as media consumption patterns change, a clutter of entertainment opportunities exist, and audience attention spans continue to shorten.

Sports with aggressive strategies to attract younger fans should be applauded. However, in the sponsorship sales process, many properties use millennial marketing programs, young social media influencers, or an esports strategy as a way to make their older audience seem younger. Since return-on-investment is measured in results today, sponsors must evaluate property audiences in the here and now. Today's audience is an indicator of potential sponsorship success, and not the aspirations of a different audience tomorrow.

CHAPTER 3

PROPERTY POTENTIAL IMPACT

I started my sports marketing career at a property. From that experience, I understand the pressure to develop sponsorship revenue as quickly as possible. During this phase of my career, I learned how the brutal sponsorship sales market could expose my property's every weakness. Over time, it became clear that veteran sponsorship managers size up properties in the first 60 seconds. They taught me what sponsors value most and what they do not value at all. However, the most important lesson I learned was "don't go to market before your property is ready."

In any given week, a sponsorship manager may receive dozens or even hundreds of sponsorship proposals. Selecting a partner is a daunting task. Questions abound in this process, including the availability of budget, the suitability of the sponsorship to the sponsor's brand, and the ability of the sponsorship to produce valuable return on investment.

However, make no mistake, sponsorship is a buyer's market. Because there are more seekers than buyers, the onus is on the property to maximize their attractiveness in the marketplace. If a property can stand out as offering great value, it will improve its chances of finding a great partner.

Does your property stand out?

In the pages that follow, I identify several factors that make a property valuable for sponsorship. Brands may use this information to distinguish good partners from not-so-good partners. These factors underscore the impact that a property can have in delivering value to the brand's sponsorship.

Properties may choose to use this chapter as a "sponsorship readiness test." Every property must engage in the pre-selling prep needed to succeed in this buyer's market. Failure to do so is like entering the Boston Marathon without a day's worth of training. Use the following checklist to start your training regimen.

The Property Impact Checklist

The checklist is tailored to properties that operate events as opposed to non-event forms of sponsorship. However, it can be modified to virtually any property seeking sponsorship. For example, I modify this checklist for not-for-profits that seek sponsorship for programs, as opposed to events.

To evaluate the potential impact of a property on a sponsorship, the following items can be considered:

✓ Attendance

- ✓ Broadcast viewership
- ✓ Market size
- ✓ Social media engagement
- ✓ Marketing plan
- ✓ Dedicated sponsorship staff
- ✓ Access to research

I will unpack this checklist to better explain property impact.

The Checklist Unpacked

ATTENDANCE

Within the sponsorship community, there is debate about whether attendance is a meaningful indicator of sponsorship health. If you divide attendance figures by the sponsorship cost divided by one thousand, you will arrive at a cost-per-thousand (CPM) figure. CPMs are commonly used to evaluate many forms of marketing activity. However, some sponsorship experts feel that CPM should not be one of them. I agree with those experts, since CPM ignores the multiplier impact of image transfer, explained in the next chapter.

For now, I am not using attendance figures to gauge the viability of a sponsorship. I recommend using attendance as one indicator of event or property impact. It is logical to argue that the impact of the property may be directly proportional to the size of the event it promotes. But there is more to attendance figures than this simple evaluation point, so I will unpack this issue further.

Like any data point, there are several important sponsorship issues that underlie the raw attendance figure. Some address the health of the event and its ability to drive brand awareness. Other issues speak to the audience that attends the event.

Some attendance questions both brands and properties should consider are:

How does attendance at this event compare to similar events? A Fourth of July concert in a small Indiana town cannot compare to the Fourth of July on the National Mall in Washington, D.C. However, I can compare it to similar summer holiday events around the Midwest. Brands can use similar comparisons to gauge relative impact and value.

Has attendance at this event been growing or contracting? This seems obvious relative to property impact. A growing event can increase brand awareness for the sponsor. I emphasize it here because of the countless times I have seen brands not request or challenge this information from properties.

What is the rate of attendance growth? This issue has been arising more often as brands include performance metrics in their sponsorship agreements. Growth has important ramifications not only in sponsorship renewal, but in any request for increased fees. I include it here as an indicator of the relative impact that a property's event can make relative to growth momentum.

What is the rate of ticket renewal year-over-year? Events

grow when a property attracts **new** attendees year over year. However, if event attendees do not renew season tickets or do not return to an event, the property must replace this lost attendee **and** find new attendees in order to grow. This double effort is known as "event churn." Sponsors may be concerned about two aspects of event churn. When there is a substantial rate of event churn, the event may not be satisfying to attendees. Additionally, if the marketing department needs to replace its audience each year, there may be less time to promote sponsorships.

If the property is a sell-out, when does it do so? A property that sells out prior to an event has reason to brag. However, a property that sells out shortly after opening ticket sales (assuming sales are many months before the event) is in the driver seat in terms of sponsorship discussions with brands. That property's audience is avid and loyal, which excites many prospective sponsors.

One final word about attendance: Many properties do not make attendance data publicly available. Additionally, there are non-ticketed events open to the public. Parades, for instance, may be difficult to assess using such data. However, despite the difficulties associated with obtaining attendance information, growth over time is an important factor in property impact.

BROADCAST VIEWERSHIP

Like attendance, broadcast viewership is not the be-all and end-all in evaluating sponsorship value or property impact.

However, accessible Wi-Fi and high-speed broadband make sponsorship properties much more attractive to buyers. Twenty years ago, a television crew needed to show up at an event with their broadcast truck. Today, with a camera and an internet connection, events can stream live on the social media platform of your choice.

There are two ways in which broadcast viewership speaks to the potential impact of a property. First, broadcast viewership serves as an indicator of the health of an event and the degree to which the event can drive sponsorship awareness. Second, brands can gauge the relative reach of their sponsored property off-site. Depending on the geographic reach of the broadcast, broadcast offers the opportunity to amplify the sponsorship message well beyond the event itself.

As is the case with attendance figures, broadcast viewership can be assessed with metrics that document comparisons to similar properties, year-over-year increases or decreases in total viewership, as well as the rate of growth. Specifically, a growth or decline in radio, TV, or streaming audiences is important to consider for a sponsorship. Of course, this raises issues about potential integration of a sponsor into the event. These factors include broadcast sponsorship, advertising on broadcast, on-site signage (which appears on camera), or other branded integrations at the event.

MARKET SIZE

A property may be evaluated by the size of its market area. In many situations, the Nielsen Designated Market

Area (DMA) list provides good basic data in this regard. The Nielsen DMA list ranks markets by the number of TV homes, with 210 markets as large as New York City metro and as small as Glendive, Montana.

However, a brand should be careful not to consider only the physical market of an event. For many special events, attendees will travel hundreds of miles across DMAs to visit a property. An attendee who is loyal enough to travel that distance should be considered as a brand examines DMAs in which the property has impact.

DIGITAL AND SOCIAL MEDIA ENGAGEMENT

Today, it is common for a property to provide a sponsor with digital exposure via the property's website. This exposure usually comes through recognition on a "partners" webpage, banner ads or other forms of rotating advertisement, or organic content. This type of online interactivity with potential audiences positively influences their awareness of and satisfaction with the sponsor's brand.[21] In other words, the same laws that impact positive outcomes for sponsors in the terrestrial world work in the digital world as well.

Additionally, research has confirmed a positive, significant association between sponsorship and social media.[22] Social media activities create authentic and organic connections with online communities, which enables positive image transfer.

This same research also found that the most effective form of social media activity was indirect. That is, social media activity originating from the property about the sponsor was considered more effective than when it originated from the sponsor. Again, third-party validation seems to apply in social media just as it does in other marketing channels.

This puts a premium on the property's ability to manage social media for the sponsor's benefit. But this does not diminish the importance of how a brand activates its sponsorship through social media. A brand must still promote its sponsorship in all relevant marketing channels – including digital and social – without losing sight of the property's social media programs as well.

I use the following questions to evaluate the property's impact via social media:

Is the property managing social media platforms relevant to the brand? For B2C brands, a property should already be engaging in some combination of Twitter, Facebook, Instagram, Snapchat, TikTok, Pinterest, and any new platforms. The amount of attention devoted to each channel would depend on the property's audience and business goals.

How many followers does the property have on each platform? While collective followings may or may not be relevant, it also important to compare its social media clout to similar properties. I would note that this is a useful metric, but it is far from the final one. Unfortunately, some brand managers take this to an irrational extreme, deeming one property more valuable than another strictly based on its number of Twitter followers.

What is the current nature of the property's social media program? For example, a brand would look at posting frequency and post quality. It would be appropriate to evaluate how the property engages with its audience – especially on behalf of its sponsors. Has the property created organic content related to its current sponsors? This type of content would certainly have more resonance than a mere re-post of the sponsor's own content.

What is the level of engagement that the property enjoys? A brand should look at the likes and re-posts by property followers. Additionally, the brand should examine the engagement rate. That is, the number of likes/comments/shares divided by the audience size each year. This will enable the brand to see growth, or lack thereof, in an apples-to-apples way year-over-year.

In addition to the creation of great content, is the property actively managing its social media program? For instance, does the property boost any of its posts or otherwise engage in social advertising? Does the property use a volunteer or part-time staff to create social media or is it handled by professionals? Additionally, does the property carry on a two-way dialogue with its community? Properties that relate to their audiences via expertly created social often do a better job of carrying the sponsor's message to that audience.

In terms of ROI, does the property have case studies highlighting achievements on behalf of its sponsors on social media? Ten years ago, when social media was a marketing add-on or after-thought, companies may not have had strong documentation of its sponsorship value. But today, there are many examples of social media driving awareness or purchase intent for sponsors. Detailing great results from past sponsorship campaigns demonstrates a strong presence in this very important marketing channel.

MARKETING PLAN QUALITY

In my experience, brands often give properties a "pass" in this area – for multiple reasons. First, it is difficult to truly assess the quality of a marketing plan for someone else's business, especially if that business is outside one's knowledge domain. A consumer-packaged goods (CPG) marketing professional should be careful in evaluating the marketing plan of a minor league baseball team, as the marketing challenges are vastly different. Anyone who has ever tried to sell a ticket to a sports event knows how incredibly hard it is.

Second, properties cannot or will not share key performance indicators with the prospect brand for reasons of confidentiality. For example, a property would not disclose its annual gross revenue or net income. Similarly, it may not disclose attendance data, even if that would help the sponsor better evaluate the sponsorship opportunity. Typically, one would evaluate the efficacy of a marketing plan through revenue growth, increasing attendance, or other internal data points. When brands do not have access to this information, it is difficult to evaluate whether the marketing plan works or not.

Despite the challenges with discerning good from not-so-good, brands should make their best determination in this area. Sometimes verifying that the property has a marketing plan at all is worth the effort.

Why?

A logo on a website or title of an event is a static representation of a sponsorship partnership. If the property and your sponsorship sit dormant, it never realizes its full potential. The degree to which the property uses its marketing bullhorn will determine whether the sponsorship relationship is activated and brought to life.

DEDICATED SPONSORSHIP STAFF

This aspect of property quality is difficult to access. A large property, like the NFL, NBA, or NASCAR, may have dozens of persons dedicated to sponsor service. A small not-for-profit may have no personnel dedicated to this purpose. Therefore, it would not be appropriate to judge a property by the size of its sponsorship service staff.

With that said, a small property cannot use its size as an excuse for poor sponsor service. Regardless of size, there must be a staff member whose job responsibilities include servicing sponsors. A great deal of effort goes into successful sponsorships, including meeting leverage deadlines, providing post-event reports, and building project plans.

Because sponsorships are about relationships, if no one is dedicated to building the relationship, how can it flourish commercially? Sponsorships also are labor-intensive.

Whether it is approving logos for use in promotional campaigns, coordinating details for a complex activation at an event, or reporting obligations of the impact of the sponsorship, these activities take time and effort.

If a sponsor cannot identify the resources within a property to properly tend to the relationship, there is a high likelihood that it will not achieve the goals first envisioned. This speaks to the issue of property quality.

ACCESS TO RESEARCH

Large brands usually have access to copious amounts of research. However, as marketing dollars get scarcer, it is important to be efficient and good stewards of marketing resources. Generally, it is good for a sponsor and its property partner to pool as much data and research as possible within the bounds of confidentiality.

Unfortunately, politics and poor business practices sometimes get in the way. An underperforming property may choose to hide damaging results from its sponsor partner. Or the property may not be experienced enough to know what data its sponsor partner values.

It is a good practice to specify upfront whether the brand will have access to the property's research about its audience and events. During the early stages of a sponsorship relationship, including negotiation, it is a good idea to ask the property whether the sponsor could have access to its non-confidential research. In some cases, even with brands that are well-funded, the property has access to research that the brand could never replicate. Properties that allow their sponsor partners to access research are more valuable to the sponsor.

Be Ready to Sell

The single most common strategy fail in the sponsorship arena is that a property can immediately start selling sponsorship regardless of property strength or comparative market conditions. Typically, a new property executive will take the reins of an organization, examine the profit and loss statement and declare, "Oh my . . . why is the sponsorship revenue so low!? Call my head of sales! We can remedy this immediately!" This hypothetical property has an abysmal website, a paltry social media audience, a non-existent public relations presence, missing CSR initiatives, and an ill-defined audience.

An important rule of sponsorship sales is "first you market, then you sell." You must do everything to make your property brand as strong as possible because sponsors have choices. A sponsorship manager at a large brand may receive hundreds of proposals in a week. Competition in this industry is as intense and cutthroat as any other industry, perhaps more so.

Properties that are not ready to sell sponsorship need to first focus on the marketing initiatives that will make the property a success. Then, they need to execute on those initiatives as well as possible. In the hypothetical above, the property should then look at the quality of its website and web traffic, its social media engagement rate, and the growing number of attendees as a sign of property brand strength in the sponsorship sales process. However, properties must be **ready** to sell, **then** sell.

Be a Consultative Partner

In my experience, properties fall into one of three broad categories. First, there are the weak properties that barely (or do not) provide the minimum level of asset fulfillment. Usually, these properties are understaffed or assign sponsorship service to entry-level employees. Second, there are the good properties that thoroughly fulfill their contractual requirements. They walk around with clipboards, ticking off each promised inventory item to ensure the sponsor gets what they pay for. Finally, there are the great properties. They are "consultative partners." Let me break down what it takes for every property to be a great collaborative partner.

Like many professionals, sponsorship managers have limited time to devote to any given sponsorship. All of us work and understand that the emergency d'jour generally gets the most management attention. Yet, the challenges of building great sponsorship programs for each property never disappear.

The sponsorship manager probably knows his or her brand better than the property. However, the property knows its brand and audience best. Thus, it is incumbent on the property to learn as much as they can about each of its sponsors and their marketing challenges. When the property considers itself one of the sponsor's marketing consultants, the likelihood of continuous improvement and value creation in the relationship increases exponentially. Consulting can take place in the following ways:

1. Suggesting new ways to leverage the property
2. Providing constructive feedback on how to improve current leverage and activation activities
3. Informing the sponsor proactively on changes in the behavior / attitudes of the property's audience
4. Offering best practices data and advice from other sponsors involved in the property
5. Sharing useful news or business information relevant to the sponsorship manager's duties and challenges
6. Communicating on a regular basis about the status of programs and opportunities
7. Networking with other sponsors to develop future programs with the property.

This type of consultative partnership positively transforms relationships. In the mind of the sponsor, the property becomes more than a "vendor" to whom a check is cut regularly. The property becomes part of the brand's marketing team in the truest sense. Finally, the property benefits from how the sponsorship is embedded in the brand's integrated marketing plan.

The Helpfulness Factor

Properties run the gamut. Some properties have sophisticated sponsorship management staff, subscribe to the right audience data services, and demonstrate creativity and flexibility on a regular basis. Other properties, not so much.

Because sponsorships are, by definition, relationships, sponsors often evaluate their partner properties by their degree of helpfulness. But, helpfulness in what areas? In a recent sponsor survey,[23] sponsors viewed the following property assistance as "valuable": assistance in measuring return on investment, post-event reports sent for fulfillment audits, audience research on attitude and image, and leveraging ideas.

Assistance with leveraging ideas has been an area of interest for me for some time. For many years, I have seen professional sports franchises (i.e., NBA, MLB, NFL, or NHL) and independent event facilities (i.e., music centers or racetracks) court local or regional retail chains as sponsorship partners. These brand partners have marketing teams skilled at their core function: selling goods or services through advertisements, point-of-purchase promotions, or social media. However, these marketers may not deal with sponsorship often.

In the mid-level and smaller-dollar sponsorship markets, properties also lack access to creative marketing services aligned with their sponsorship sales. The result is that both parties would like to entertain sponsorship, but do not know how to build one that benefits both sides. For this reason, some sponsorship deals do not work out because they cannot agree on ways in which the brand can leverage and activate the sponsorship.

Recognizing this gap in the sponsorship sales process, properties are increasingly including leverage ideas in sponsorship proposals. The survey referenced above noted that a growing number of sponsors found this tactic to be valuable. In some cases, providing leverage ideas as part a sponsorship proposal may be the difference between closing a deal and not closing one.

While sponsors appreciate this assistance and find it helpful, properties should not ignore the downside of this sponsorship sales strategy. Even if you were to stamp "confidential" all over your sponsorship proposal, and put a copyright sign on it, an idea is not a protectable intellectual property asset. An unscrupulous brand or its agency may end up using an unprotected great idea in a competing sponsorship. It has happened to me. Over the years, I have found the following tips useful in protecting your valuable ideas:

- Do not send leverage ideas in every case. Use this tactic selectively.
- Send ideas only to brands with good reputations and a history of collaboration.
- Do not send leverage ideas in the first communication with a brand. Simply indicate that ideas would be forthcoming if the brand expresses actual interest in a dialogue.

However, do not let the fear of being duped cause you to avoid this technique. Leveraging ideas is still a valuable strategy that should not be ignored.

CHAPTER 4

IMAGE TRANSFER: SPONSORSHIP'S SUPERPOWER

Why Do We Care?

When I think of the Chicago Cubs, certain images and associations come to mind. I associate the Cubs with (mostly) exciting baseball, a sport that I have appreciated since my father took my brother and I to a New York Mets game. As a child, I lived near the Mets' Shea Stadium in Queens, which is a strong memory as well. Attending games at Wrigley Field, I appreciate the nostalgic feel of a stadium built for the game's intimate enjoyment.

Within the "Friendly Confines" (also a nickname meant to generate an association), I can remember a refreshing Old Style Beer and a delicious Chicago Dog. However, my strongest association involves the memory of special weekends spent with my sons on Chicago trips, all built around a Cubs victory or two at the ballpark.

And I am not the only one with strong positive images and associations of the Chicago Cubs. Billions of people have similarly impactful associations related to a favorite sports team, a music festival, a great museum, or an important nonprofit cause. These associations drive us to attend events, watch event videos, and make substantial financial contributions from our disposable income.

Now, imagine that you could tap into all that emotional power. What would you do if you could capture emotional energy and transfer it for productive use? What could you accomplish?

Those of us who work in sponsorship know exactly what that power looks like. This "superpower" of sponsorship, called "image transfer," has been verified by research. Let me unpack what it means and how you can leverage it to create powerful associations.

Remember my associations related to the Chicago Cubs? Image transfer describes "the transfer of such associations to a brand or company sponsoring this activity."[24] Sponsorship "frequently generates a favorable image for the sponsor, both at the corporate and brand levels."[25] It is when a positive association from a property rubs off on the brand. If I view the Chicago Cubs as professionals who win baseball games and make valuable family memories happen, I will view their sponsors as winners who care about families. In its simplest form, that is how image transfer works.

There have been attempts to verify image transfer and explain why it happens and how to make it happen more effectively. Existing research is consistent with my experience, including work in both sponsorship and athlete endorsements.

Image transfer in sponsorship originated from research discussions about celebrity endorsement. It involves the following theory of marketing, where marketing intersects with psychology and sociology:

> It is argued that consumers view products as bundles of utility that satisfy functional needs but also as collections of meanings that service to constitute who they are. Belongings are regarded as part of ourselves and enable us to acquire or reinforce our self-identities. Thus, brand consumption has developed into a process of self-identity and self-expression that facilitates self-enhancement. Consumers search the material world for products with certain meanings of gender, social status, age, personality traits, and psychographics and are constantly appropriating products' symbolic attributes to create traits of their self-concept.[26] (citations omitted)

This theory of "meaning transfer" explains why celebrity endorsement works. We buy products endorsed by celebrities who stand for the cultural meanings that we desire in our own lives. If I buy an Omega watch, perhaps I will be more like its endorser, George Clooney.[27] At least this is what I think subconsciously.

Researchers have suggested that image transfer works the same way in sponsorship.[28] Sponsored activities, like Cubs baseball games, have positive associations, personality, and aura attributed to them. As in the case of George Clooney, I will associate other positive attributes to Cubs' sponsors. This is especially true if I assume that the sponsors are supporting the Cubs for some benevolent reason. Perhaps the sponsor is making stadium Wi-Fi possible, creating more entertainment opportunities at the event, or just supplying the beer. Image transfer is particularly effective in smaller events, too. From a revenue perspective, sponsors are sometimes responsible for making an entire event possible, like a local 10K race, which engenders appreciation from the audience.

Image transfer and positive associations underscore how sponsorship can be more powerful than advertising. In advertising, the audience knows that the brand is trying to sell them something. So, customers put up a force field of skepticism when encountering these messages. However, when the audience views the brand as a benefactor, it is viewed more favorably.[29] "The consumer may even feel the need or desire to reciprocate by purchasing the brand."[30]

While on the topic of advertising, image transfer offers another sponsorship advantage. Advertising messages generally originate from the brand itself. But with sponsorship, the positive image transferred to the brand is akin to third-party validation. The property is giving the brand its "objective" seal of approval.

Sponsors hope that a more favorable image leads to purchase intention. If sponsors look at their marketing and sales process as moving consumers from awareness to consideration to purchase, they want sponsorship to help consumers pull the trigger. In its simplest form, image transfer enables marketers to shortcut the brand-building process by using another brand's positive imagery to its own advantage.

Before I discuss the practical reasons why image transfers works (or does not), I would be remiss if I didn't mention several other mechanisms that benefit brands through sponsorship.[31]

- Sponsorship creates simple awareness. Repeated exposure to the sponsor during an event creates a positive effect in the mind of the consumer. However, an over-commercialized message, as I'll discuss below, can have the opposite impact.
- Through "affect transfer," a positive feeling can be transferred from a property to a sponsor as a result of the sponsorship relationship.
- There can be a benefit of "affiliation," where the consumer feels the brand's products or services are "made for people like me" as a result of the sponsorship.
- There is the benefit of "implied size," where if the audience believes the sponsor is big time, then the event is big time. The opposite can hold true as well, where a large event enhances the reputation of a smaller sponsor.

- Interestingly, there is the benefit of reciprocity. If the audience believes the sponsor's support has made their event possible or more enjoyable, they feel compelled to support the sponsor with a purchase. I have experienced this directly in auto racing, where sponsorship is the lifeblood of the business model. No sponsors, no racing. And the fans know it.

Clearly, sponsorship offers a variety of benefits, but from a strategic perspective, I will continue to focus on image transfer. It is the most valuable theory explaining why sponsorship impacts consumers emotionally. Emotion is where the magic happens.

What Drives Image Transfer?

Those who have studied image transfer empirically have identified several important conditions that impact the ability to transfer image, both positively and negatively. These include (1) sponsorship fit, (2) commercialization, (3) sincerity or authenticity, and (4) involvement. As sponsorship strategists, our goal is to align these qualities to maximize positive image transfer. I will discuss these moderators one at a time.

SPONSORSHIP FIT

It is logical to assume that when a sports fan arrives at a stadium, he or she may look at a sponsor logo and process it either consciously or unconsciously: "Does it make sense that this sponsor is involved in this event?" If there is a "logical relationship and connection," the fan accepts the sponsor's presence and can readily process the connection.[32] Key impact potential is whether the sponsorship makes sense and whether it is expected, or not surprising, to the consumer.[33] Multiple studies show that a more coherent sponsorship results in a more effective sponsorship.

"Fit" has been defined in two ways: category fit and personality fit. For category fit, the sponsorships line up in the same category. For instance, categories could include sports events, art festivals, or social causes. Personality fit involves sponsorships that have similar personal attributes. For example, sponsorships that share similar personalities may include the X Games and EDC Las Vegas (electronic dance music) because both are perceived as exciting and uninhibited.

Sponsor event fit addresses the "why?" of the sponsorship. There is an inverse correlation between perceived commercial goals and image enhancement. The more commercial fans perceive the sponsor, the less they hold the sponsor in high regard. Endemic sponsors in any sport know this. There is no problem with a motor oil company showing up at an auto racing event. However, when a mortgage finance company tags along, there may be questions about issue fit.

The sponsorship industry often blends "natural fit" with the terms "endemic" and "non-endemic" sponsors. Endemic sponsors "generally refers to the core group of brands on which a sport relies," usually the manufacturers of products used in the sport.[34] In motorsports, endemic sponsors make the cars run; engine suppliers like Honda, Chevy, and Ford; motor oils like Pennzoil and Mobil 1; or tires manufacturers like Firestone or Michelin. No fan of auto racing would question why Firestone sponsors the sport. It is endemic and has perfect congruence.

Non-endemic sponsors, on the other hand, are outsiders. The question then becomes to what extent do non-endemic sponsors not fit or lack congruence. In esports, for instance, computer hardware and peripheral manufacturers would clearly be endemic partners. However, what about recent entrants in the quick service restaurant, energy drinks, and snack food categories? It depends on the brand and how it communicates to the market why it fits. Several factors would predict their fit's success or failure:

- Does the non-endemic brand have a pre-existing connection with the audience? For example, does the audience currently use the brand's products or services?
- Does the non-endemic brand speak the language of the audience? For example, does the brand's message resonate with the audience demographic and/or psychographic?
- Does the non-endemic brand represent the same values as the audience? For example, if the audience cares about corporate social responsibility, is that true for the brand as well?

Admittedly, the non-endemic brand must do more to establish its fit in a new sponsorship environment. However, failure to establish this key factor will spell trouble for ROI down the road.

What happens when you ignore sponsorship fit? Whether it is personality fit or category fit, one truth remains: Fit cannot be fudged. As the adage goes, "if the shoe fits, wear it." So, if the brand fits the category or personality of the property, great!

Unfortunately, an all-too-common sponsorship pitfall involves when fit is entirely neglected. Sponsorship veterans have different nicknames for sponsorships of this type. I call them "hobby sponsorships."

These happen when a senior executive, usually the CEO or Chairman, intervenes in the company's sponsorship selection process to exercise an opinion, often on a whim. Think: The CEO who plays golf as a hobby and then wants to sponsor a golf event. Or a CMO who has long admired a certain musician and wants to integrate that talent in a sponsorship activation. Even an executive who was starstruck after meeting an NBA's teams most famous players. In all these cases, the brand's executive became an emotional buyer rather than a rational one. After a long career in sponsorship, I have seen it all.

And you can probably guess the outcome. It may be a mind-numbingly bad ROI or even the executive being terminated. However, there is another type of bad outcome. This outcome involves a failed sponsorship. Because of the bad fit, which was ignored by the hobby sponsorship, the partnership failed to produce for the brand. Rather than accept responsibility, the "decider" blames the property, or worse, blames the sport, or worse still, blames sponsorship itself as expensive and ineffective. This hurts everyone involved. And it usually starts with a whim.

Other than avoiding hobby sponsorships completely, there is only one way to combat this pitfall. You pull out the data. Lots of data. Data regarding the audience demographics compared to your brand's data. What is the statistical cohesion between the brand's audience and the property's? Data regarding audience psychographics. Will the audience welcome the brand, and do they really want or need what the brand offers?

COMMERCIALIZATION

Sponsorship works because consumers let their guards down. When that happens, fans are more likely to accept the sponsor's messages. Additionally, there is an inverse correlation between perceived commercial goals and image enhancement. The more commercial fans perceive the sponsor, the less they hold the sponsor in high regard.

This is a delicate balance. If a baseball sponsor chooses to run their normal TV commercial spot on the big screen between innings, what will the audience think? They will assume you are trying to sell them something. But what if that same sponsor runs a spot about their support of the baseball team's outreach program for disadvantaged kids?

The audience probably appreciates that the sponsor is making their community a better place to live.

In the face of pressure to yield better outcomes, sponsor managers and their agencies often have to make tough choices. But crossing the line of commercialization impedes positive image transfer from the property.

The easiest way to not act commercially is to behave benevolently. Sports executive Rod Davis, CEO of Davis Sports & Entertainment, puts it this way:

> The purpose of sponsorship is to engage and have a 1:1 conversation. How do I take this relationship that I have with the property and make the fan's experience better? How do I take my platform and deliver them added value? And when I make their experience better at that event, concert or game, then I've connected with them, I've earned their trust and their respect. They are going to tell their friends how great this thing was and that gives me permission to market to them.[35]

AUTHENTICITY AND SINCERITY

Sponsor sincerity also creates a strategic challenge for brands. It puts a premium on "understanding the attitudes held about their event by their audience and by those in the population who see their event as important."[36] For sponsors to achieve positive brand association, "they must be perceived as sincere enablers of activities that benefit both the activity audience and community at large rather than just purely commercially-oriented events."[37]

The key here is to demonstrate that the sponsor is involved for the audience's benefit. This requires communicating the authentic reasons why a brand chooses to sponsor a property. They may be obvious, but they should also be articulated. For instance, we see many large companies purchase naming rights as stadium title sponsors. If such a sponsorship is motivated by the fact that the sponsor is headquartered the stadium's city, that should be communicated often. In this case, the benefit to the fan is a new state-of-the-art facility to enjoy their favorite team.

Sincerity addresses the issue of motive. Is the sponsor here to sell more stuff or is the sponsor here to enhance the event and the fan experience? This requires a balancing act internal to the brand's sponsorship team. For example, if a brand promotes the sales of its products or services with the sponsorship, the sponsor may appear overtly commercial.[38]

Similarly, research encourages the sponsor to *not* enforce its contractual rights of exclusivity against ambushers. Rather, the property should do this dirty work to allow the sponsor to appear less commercially motivated.[39] The more the sponsor can communicate its sincerity to benefit the consumer, the more image benefit the sponsor will enjoy.

Conversely, certain activities can negatively impact perceived sincerity. For example, if the sponsor runs a sales promotion as part of the sponsorship. If done in an overtly commercial way, it will undercut its sincerity and benevolent motives. And sometimes, when sponsors jump on high-profile events, the audience will perceive the sponsorship to be motivated by selfish goals.[40] If a sponsor is driven by a sincere desire to benefit the audience, that should guide sales promotions and other activities.

INVOLVEMENT

All event attendees are not alike. Some are avid fans who cheer for the home team every game. Others attend events to relate to friends and family or are tag-alongs, just there for the ride. These audience members have different levels of involvement with a sponsored event. And research tells us this involvement has a moderating effect on image transfer.[41]

Event involvement is "a kind of genuine excitement caused by a strong and solid interest in a specific activity."[42] Fans who are more engaged in events are "more likely to respond positively to the sponsorship activities."[43] It is relevant to note that there is no singular activity that makes one attendee more involved than another. For example, an avid sports fan may be involved because he is a stats junkie. But a concert goer who is excited to see her friends at a venue can be just as involved. It does not really matter why audiences attend events; it matters how engaged they are. "Strong and solid interest" is the key differentiator.

Image transfer works better for involved attendees because their interest causes them to pay greater attention to sponsor messages. Sponsor benefits are also stronger among those who are heavily involved, as they are generally "opinion leaders and are heavy buyers with better responses to promotional activities."[44]

Image Transfer in Multi-Sponsorship Portfolios

So far, I have focused on the impact that one sponsorship has on brand equity transfer. But other research correlates a brand's sponsorship portfolio with its image. The fit between individual sponsorship properties within a broader sponsorship portfolio can also impact consumer perceptions of the sponsor's brand image.[45] If consumers perceive a fit, brand image is strengthened. Conversely, a lack of fit has been shown to weaken the sponsor's brand image.

This can be a distressing finding to the managers of large corporate sponsorship portfolios. However, it may also impact smaller sponsors, including a variety of regional hospital health care systems who may use sponsorship for community relations purposes as opposed to marketing ones.

This dynamic becomes more complex when companies have multiple sponsorship properties divided among multiple product brands. For example, automakers have unique brand strategies related to each of their car models, while a snack brand, like Frito-Lay, has different brand considerations for products as diverse as Tostitos, Rold Gold pretzels, and Cracker Jack.

Strategically, there are two countermeasures to this sponsorship portfolio dilemma. The first and most obvious countermeasure is to create a portfolio with sponsorships that align on a category or personality level. Ideally, the category or personality align with the brand attributes of the sponsor. Hobby sponsorships that are picked based on an executive's passions should be a big red flag.

Second, if the consistency of a portfolio is not intuitive, the portfolio manager should communicate the shared traits of each sponsorship – through words or imagery. In the process, the manager can create more brand benefit describing the "why" of the sponsorship portfolio.

"It Matters Who You Stand on Stage With"

I am fortunate to have friends much smarter than me. One of those friends frequently cites that adage, "It matters who you stand on stage with." The premise of this quote is you want to be on stage with people who make you look good through association. Interestingly, the same concept applies in sponsorship. A 2013 study found that, in a multi sponsor environment within a single property's sponsor roster, there is brand image transfer between sponsors.[46] In other words, the positive or negative image of one sponsor can impact others in the environment.

Sponsors considered prestigious may want to align together. This has practical applications, especially for sponsors that wish to engage in B2B activities with their peers.

Additionally, sponsors that wish to appear prestigious may benefit from other big names in the crowd.

In order to facilitate this process, sponsorship managers have two options. First, they should first confirm the identity of any other sponsors. Second, a sponsor with significant bargaining power should want to retain veto rights over subsequent new sponsors. Admittedly, this veto right may be difficult to win in negotiations. Nonetheless, the risk of negative brand image transfer exists, and pre-emptively protecting a sponsor from it is a wise strategy.

Practical Approaches to Boost Image Transfer

Now that I have laid a lot of research on you, it is time to explore some practical approaches to take advantage of sponsorship's greatest gift, image transfer. There are several approaches that take place in the sponsorship building phase, while other strategies are more applicable in the sponsorship implementation phase. Below, I will discuss both.

WHEN EVALUATING A SPONSORSHIP

Just because a brand and a property share a target audience does not mean that the two are congruent or a good fit in the eyes of consumers. In evaluating a sponsorship, you should consider the following:

1. Former partners of the property. Do they align with the new partnership? Do they have the same status to consumers?

2. The voice of the property. Do they share the same voice of the brand? Social media feeds are the quickest way to ascertain whether there is alignment in this area. I also see a starkest contrast of this in sports. A property that is rowdy or brags would not be a good fit for a passive brand with a humble brand personality.

3. The CSR stance of the property. Do they have a similar attitude towards CSR and giving back to the community?

4. The respective ownership groups of the brand and the property. If they had dinner together, would they get along?

5. The roster of co-sponsors. I mentioned above the importance of "it matters who you stand on stage with." This is the time to evaluate other partners.

Certainly, there are subjective elements to this evaluation, I admit. It is hard to measure voice. However, if you feel your brand lacks the objectivity to evaluate the question of fit, ask your consumers. Surveys, focus groups, and social listening all provide clues to fit from your customer's perspective. Use the tools that make your business successful to allow the customer to decide if a brand fits a certain property.

WHEN BUILDING A SPONSORSHIP PORTFOLIO

Few sponsorship managers have the luxury of cultivating a large, multi-sponsorship portfolio from scratch. Often, a manager inherits a hodge-podge of legacy deals cultivated over many years with input of numerous executives, some of whom are no longer with the organization. When looking at such portfolios, one is reminded of the musical *Joseph and the Amazing Technicolor Dreamcoat*: a blinding array of beautiful, expensive, and unrelated sponsorships.

I often see this conundrum in the health care industry. Wanting to cultivate strong relationships with the community, regional health care systems get committed to a bundle of unrelated, yet deserving, sponsorship properties. Of course, it does not help that the CEO sits on numerous community boards where he or she is hit up frequently for sponsorship. Each morning, this organization's sponsorship manager arrives at work with a new sponsorship sitting on their desk, and the habit adds up over time.

In such cases, I recommend getting back to basics. Pick a theme or multiple themes that align with your key brand goals. Using fit as your guide, religiously thin the herd. Line up the expiration dates of sponsorships and determine which fit and which do not. Renew the sponsorships that fit your themes. Let the ones that do not expire. As you move forward, you have the opportunity to implement a more coherent and powerful theme.

Gatorade is as a great example of a consistent portfolio. This product was developed at the University of Florida by a football team for a football team. Its product properties of replenishing the fluids, electrolytes, and carbohydrates connects it inextricably to game play. For its many athlete, team, and league sponsorships, Gatorade ensures that its relationships always connect it to competition and the field of play. Its classic Gatorade barrel and the "Gatorade shower" that celebrate victory underscore this theme no matter the sport or the sponsorship.

WHEN BUILDING THE IMPLEMENTATION PLAN

As I explore throughout this book, a sponsorship implementation plan is where great strategy meets impressive tactics. It hits the consumer with a variety of impactful tactics timed for maximum effect.

After the euphoria of the new sponsorship announcement begins to fade, a brand's sponsorship team should begin to plot the leverage strategy. Ideally, this was done before the announcement. However, after a few decades of this work, I am a realist. Many sponsors plan for the sponsorship after the relationship is formed. Regardless of when the implementation plan is completed, managing two elements of image transfer will increase its effectiveness: sponsor event fit and sponsor sincerity.[47]

As discussed earlier in this chapter, a sponsor either fits or it does not. By the time you get to a leverage strategy, fit has been established. However, when building an implementation plan, it is vital that the sponsor explicitly or implicitly communicate fit. By articulating the reasons behind the sponsorship, the property will reinforce its awareness among audiences. For example, when announcing its Kentucky Derby sponsorship, Ford Motor Company noted in its press release that Ford's connections to the historic race existed on multiple levels: both brands were synonymous with freedom, Ford's products were often used during horse racing events, and Ford built pickup trucks in Kentucky.[48]

If sponsor fit is not obvious, create messages that express it. Above, I referenced endemic sponsors in auto racing. There is practically no challenge in communicating why an engine oil company is a racing sponsor. A mortgage company presents more of a challenge. In this case, the mortgage company could express the following:

- Many of its customers are racing fans, so it wants to support the event
- One of the company's founders was a race car driver in his youth, so he wants to give back to the sport
- The event has high economic impact; it wants to support community growth
- The company is helping one of its official charities through the sponsorship, creating a benefit to the community

As I noted above, sincerity and commercialization are inversely related. In other words, you will look insincere if you have crassly commercial motives. This can take many forms, but some sponsors get hung up on sales promotion. Here are a few examples:

- The sponsor's onsite display is simply a sales display with no fan benefit
- Fans receive email solicitations because they bought tickets

The sponsor offers the same discount to fans that it offers to the general public

On the flip side, here are several examples that have balanced sincerity and commercialization well:

- Coupons or discounts for attendees only
- Free products or services for attendees only
- On-site displays communicating features and benefits while also providing an experiential benefit for the attendee

Sponsors and properties can also develop strategies to increase audience involvement in the event. These strategies can be aimed at satisfying very involved fans, increasing involvement for less-engaged fans, or both.

For those attendees with higher levels of involvement, consider strategies meant to stoke their passions:

- Engage in leverage activities steeped in statistics or event history. Consider event trivia or history contests, throwback-era promotions, sponsoring the team app, or providing more data archives online
- Offer more behind-the-velvet-ropes opportunities for highly involved audiences. Think about fan meet-and-greets either at the event or online, or special autograph sessions
- Create direct relationships with athletes, celebrities, or artists. Through player endorsements, demonstrate team connection and commitment.

For those attendees who are less engaged, consider these strategies to increase their level of involvement:

- Support specific CSR activities that have broad community applicability. Consider supporting a local charity at the event or carrying their message as part of the sponsor's event messaging

- Create opportunities for "introductions" to the sport of event. Hold "Fan 101" briefings to make the sport or event more accessible to new attendees.

- Provide more generalized benefits that enhance the overall fan experience. These may include product giveaways, ancillary entertainment opportunities, or free Wi-Fi.

CHAPTER 5

WHAT MAKES A GOOD SPONSOR PARTNER?

In the preceding chapters, I outlined the characteristics of a good property. These characteristics impact the sponsorship benefit formula. However, from a property perspective, it is also important to consider the qualities of a good sponsor. Because the sponsorship relationship is a two-way street, having a good sponsor increases the likelihood of good marketing outcomes.

There are no hard and fast rules that make a sponsor a good partner. But my experience has generated a great deal of insight. Below, I identify criteria that I have found to promote healthy and productive relationships between brands and properties. They are issues that could be managed as part of the business experience to build more powerful sponsorships together.

THE SPONSOR HAS EXPERIENCE REGARDING HOW SPONSORSHIPS WORK

Larger consumer brands know their way around sponsorships. Often, these brands are led by sponsorship veterans with years of valuable experience and substantial teams of dedicated sponsorship marketers. In the US, there may be about 200 sponsors of this size and level of expertise.

More often, sponsors will be smaller companies without a dedicated sponsorship staff. Their marketing teams are responsible for a wider of array of marketing responsibilities including advertising, public relations, or digital marketing. For these businesses, sponsorship is not something they do every day. These brands know that sponsorship alignment will create value, but they may not be sure what kind of value or how to create it.

During the sales process with a less experienced sponsor, I recommend slowing things down. When an inexperienced brand goes into a sponsorship relationship without clear expectations and a defined sense of strategy and realistic outcomes, difficulties and disagreements occur down the road. In this case, I recommend one of two possible approaches. First, the property should recommend the brand retain a sponsorship agency for guidance. Second, the property should adopt a consultative sales approach where it acts as a mentor for the brand.

THE SPONSOR HAS ENOUGH RESOURCES FOR LEVERAGE OR ACTIVATION ACTIVITIES

Sponsorships begin when the property and sponsor agree to a set of sponsorship rights and a rights fee. Great sponsorships happen when the sponsor leverages the sponsorship, bringing the relationship to life and achieving powerful results. To attain success, sponsors need time, energy, and capital beyond the rights fee.

Every property wants a sponsor with enormous financial resources to leverage the sponsorship. Realistically, the sponsor should have at least proportionate resources to leverage the sponsorship. If a sponsor can afford only $10,000 as a rights fee, the property would want to see a $10,000 budget for leverage.

No matter what the size of the sponsor's budget, a sponsor without proportionate resources to leverage the sponsorship makes for a poor partner. A sponsor without leverage plans results in an empty category. It may pay the property's bills, but in the long run, it will be dead weight.

THE BROADER SPONSOR ORGANIZATION
REALLY WANTS THE SPONSORSHIP

Let's face it: Sponsorships are hard. They require money, smart strategy, detailed planning, and excellent execution. However, the powerful results of sponsorship are directly proportionate to the level of difficulty.

When engaging in a sponsorship dialogue with a property, one or more internal champions from the brand side usually lead discussions. By the time the sponsor and the property agree to deal terms, the participants have great enthusiasm for the new relationship. However, in the case of larger sponsors, it is important that the sponsor's entire organization is aligned with the sponsorship's goals and direction.

I've seen relationships with poor alignment, and they simply are not successful – like when a sponsor's CEO failed to support the CMO's sponsorship decision. Sometimes, the sponsorship relationship begins with a CEO who builds a sponsorship deal without consulting the CMO or the staff, resulting in a negative budget impact and little-to-no say about the sponsorship. Such a lack of aligned internal support usually results in organizational dysfunction, lack of requisite commitment to a leverage plan, and generally, poor results.

For this reason, I recommend that both properties and brands familiarize themselves with their counterpart's organizations. Usually, time does not allow a comprehensive orientation pre-deal. However, both parties should not proceed forward unless each is convinced that the other is committed to the relationship.

THE SPONSOR EVIDENCES SOME
DEGREE OF FLEXIBILITY

Stuff happens. Inevitably, the circumstances around a sponsorship, like any human endeavor, are fraught with risk and unanticipated events. Sometimes inventory is destroyed or unavailable. Conflicts may arise with an event date. There may even be a public health crisis that completely disrupts events or the relationship.

The sponsorship industry has always been ruled by Murphy's Law: If it can go wrong, it will. Having a flexible partner helps build productive relationships and can turn unanticipated crises into victories instead of failures.

THE PARTIES DO NOT REQUIRE PERFECTION.
Like any set of criteria, it will be rare that a sponsor can check every box in the preceding list. However, the purpose of this chapter was to highlight that a sponsorship depends as much on great sponsors as great properties. Good things happen when both parties possess as many of these qualities as possible.

SECTION 2

UNIQUE STRATEGIES

CHAPTER 6

BUSINESS TO BUSINESS

Most of *Sponsorship Strategy* looks at using sponsorship in a business-to-consumer market. However, depending on the product or service, business-to-business activity matches or even surpasses the size of the business-to-consumer market.[49] By acknowledging the importance of business-to-business to many companies, this chapter focuses on leveraging sponsorship in these environments.

Business-to-business (B2B) refers to sales that companies make to other businesses rather than to individual consumers.[50] While the object of the sale can be a product or service, B2B is different than its business-to-consumer (B2C) counterpart in a few ways. First, the B2B buyer is usually a professional buyer or executive. Second, the selling cycle is typically longer than a B2C sale. The longer sales cycle derives from how B2B buyers must have confidence that the seller can deliver what it promises. This confidence-building process takes time.

B2B sponsors generally articulate one or more of the following goals:

1. Increase revenue
2. Create a platform for developing relationships
3. Provide an opportunity to entertain customers
4. Generate employee good will[51]

Many B2B marketers believe that events are the single most effective marketing channel, trumping digital advertising, email marketing, and content marketing.[52] There is something about the excitement of an event environment that turbo-charges buyers and sellers. In fact, during my property days, one of my sponsor partners enjoyed a 32:1 return on investment from its B2B sponsorship. Nowhere else in their sales program could they match that impact.

There are four elements to B2B sponsorship strategy that boost its effectiveness as a sales and marketing tool:

- The sponsorship enhances the sponsor's image as a prestigious partner
- Sponsorships often generate unique experiences that forge relationships with the sponsorship partner
- Sponsorships offer the opportunity to create a live-action showcase for products and services
- Sponsorship activities provide access to key decision makers

The Image of the B2B Sponsor

Many B2B sponsorship managers would tell you that revenue numbers are the beginning and end of their responsibility.

However, for every B2B sponsor that says he or she does not care about brand building, there is one that will shell out big bucks to align with a very prestigious property.

Corporations have long viewed sports sponsorships as a means of enhancing corporate image.[53] This is as true in B2B sponsorships as it is in B2C sponsorships.

Even if a company is B2B focused, a good promotion plan should be part of every sponsorship experience. It should include pre-event, event, and post-event promotions aligned with the sponsors' current marketing channels (i.e., social media, video, PR, advertising, etc.).

Finally, there is a social concern that the event includes other sponsors with similar prestige. Remember the adage, "It's important who you stand on stage with"? For this reason, a Fortune 500 B2B company may not want to co-sponsor an event with small, local businesses with whom they have little in common.

Generating Unique Experiences

In the world of B2B sponsorship, sponsors rely heavily on hospitality to facilitate the brand-property relationship. Hopefully, in the sponsorship negotiation process, the sponsor has carved out the most important part of the hospitality equation: access to unique experiences. This also represents an area where the property can provide valuable creative insight to its prospective sponsorship partner.

The buyer in the B2B process is a professional buyer or

a company executive. Even as the U.S. tax code continues to discourage deducting client entertainment, buyers often have ample opportunity to be wined-and-dined by sales professionals. It is sad to say, but many of these people are tired of eating at the best restaurants or receiving free tickets to sporting events.

Within the B2B sponsorship experience, the best sponsors create something very different. Often, it is about access. When I say access, I do not just mean an event, a club seat, or even a suite. I mean a once-in-a-lifetime, truly original experience that the guest cannot experience anywhere else. It may be a meet-and-greet with a famous athlete, a ride in a NASCAR pace car, or standing on the sideline before an NFL game.

I have seen sponsors create a variety of special access events in the context of sponsorship:

- Access to elite athletes, celebrities, artists
- Opportunities to participate in high excitement events (i.e., Golf Pro-Ams, award show receptions)
- Opportunities to participate in completely unique events (i.e., ride in an IndyCar two-seater)
- Behind-the-scenes access or special VIP tours
- Access to sold-out events

These unique once-in-a-lifetime experiences are not akin to another steakhouse dinner or one MLB game in a 162-game schedule. In this sense, access is not an afterthought. It is a strategic element that is identified and carved out at the start of a sponsorship relationship – even before the contract is signed. Its value to B2B sponsorships cannot be overstated.

Bringing Your Company to Life

B2B sponsorship managers often tell me they are "uninterested in activation." Many think of it as the consumer version of an interactive display meant to entertain or generate leads for future sales. While I may agree that the typical B2C sponsorship activation is not suited for the B2B context, there are several ways a B2B sponsor can bring its relationship to life at a sponsored event.

PRODUCT INTEGRATIONS

The most important leveraging activity, in my view, is product integration. Product integration occurs when a sponsor can incorporate a product or a service into the delivery of an event. For instance, product integrations have become very important for technology companies. The Microsoft Surface has powered NFL sidelines and NASCAR pit boxes. Intel helps power fan-friendly technology for Levi's Stadium. IBM designs and develops the digital experience of the US Open tennis championship. In nearly every circumstance, each brand benefits from the direct association with the property. These sponsors do not merely slap a logo on a sign. They help make the event possible – or at least say as much.

When a sponsor can integrate its product directly into

a sport or event, there is a significant halo effect from this display. For B2B consumers who see the product integration aligned with an event, there is significant image transfer.

LIVE DEMONSTRATIONS AND FREE SAMPLES

When it is not possible to integrate a product directly into the event, products can still be demonstrated at the event. There is no substitute for the visceral experience of seeing and feeling a product or service in action. If a fan midway is not the suitable place for such a demonstration, these activities can occur in hospitality areas or suites where potential customers can be found. For example, at running events, like the OneAmerica 500 Festival Mini-Marathon, there are any number of sponsored samples for participants: water, juices, fruit bowls, or low-carb beer.

PROMOTIONAL MERCHANDISE

If the B2B sponsorship experience is a "critical sales event," there should be some token to create a memory around the event. A branded hat, a customized co-branded team jersey, or anything worth saving should be considered as part of the B2B strategy.

At this point, are you thinking that strategy is trivial, or I strayed off in the weeds? No way. I have walked through the offices of many companies where desks and cubicles are littered with these memory tokens. This type of brand awareness helps fuel the $23 billion promotional merchandise industry.[54] So, why should this powerful tool be ignored? It shouldn't.

ATTENDEES AND KEY DECISION MAKERS

Because sponsorships and their leverage events are expensive, great care should be given to the attendee list. Having the right people from the buy and sell sides ensures maximum impact for the B2B sponsorship. Most B2B sponsorship events involve venues where key decision makers mingle among one another. No gatekeepers prevent conversations. The non-business atmosphere of the event promotes relaxed conversation. It is often the perfect place to do business.

When considering the substantial opportunities that a B2B sponsorship offers, what makes for good attendees?

The buyer's side is a delicate balance. Most sales professionals would advocate "going to power" in a typical sales discussion. The higher you get on the organization chart, the greater the prospects for success. Thus, the sales professional will do anything to get to the CEO or their colleagues in the C-suite. But this sales technique does not always work in B2B sponsorships.

In the B2B sponsorship, attendees from the buyer would include persons involved in the buying approval process and who have subject-matter expertise in the product/service area. Having a hands-off CEOs at an event does little good if that person is not a subject-matter expert. Imagine the CEO returning to the office after an event and explaining that he or she heard great things about the thing-a-ma-jig that makes the whatcha-ma-call-it work better. Not helpful. Instead, invitees from the buyer occupy strategic points in the transaction approval process.

From the seller's side, attendees should represent three key areas. First, a C-Suite attendee projects the importance of the event. Their attendance confirms that the occasion is special. Second, a sales representative creates continuity for the discussion after the event. A B2B sponsorship accelerates the sales process, and a professional should be present to capitalize on that. Third, a product/service expert should be in attendance to answer fast-ball technical questions. Many B2B deals have been derailed with the phrase, "That's a good question. I'll get back to you next week when we get back to the office."

A Word About Measurement

It may be obvious that B2B sponsorships are measured by lift in sales. Sponsors often cut right to the heart of it and demand a sales ROI as the primary measurement criterion. However, like its B2C counterpart, a B2B partnership is also measured by improvements in brand awareness or purchase consideration. As is the case generally, B2B sponsors should confirm which measures validate the sponsorship from the perspective of their overall business strategy.

Additionally, I recommend that B2B sponsors uniformly adopt a "control and test" measurement to determine the efficacy of their sponsorship hospitality. To use a control and test measure, divide your buying audience into two parts: buyers who attend a B2B sponsorship event (the

"Treated Buyer") and buyers who do not have access to such benefits (the "Untreated Buyer").

The control and test measure compares Treated Buyers to Untreated Buyers against standard sales measures used to manage the sales process. Some companies, for example, measure pipeline velocity (the speed of closing a sale), customer acquisition value, or cost of acquisition. No matter which measure is used, the B2B sponsorship can be deemed successful if Treated Buyers demonstrate higher measurable potential than Untreated Buyers. In other words, sales closed faster or closed for greater amounts because of access to B2B events. Failing to use a control and test approach just leaves you guessing about whether an expensive sponsorship hospitality yielded business dividends.

CHAPTER 7

CORPORATE SOCIAL RESPONSIBILITY

What is CSR?

Consumers increasingly appreciate a company's sense of social responsibility and have been expressing their values with their voices and wallets. For this reason, the past decade has witnessed a movement called "corporate social responsibility," or CSR. At its core, CSR is "a self-regulating business model that helps a company be socially accountable – to itself, its stakeholders and the public."[55]

With this wave of socially conscious capitalism, companies create formal CSR policies as part of their corporate governance and even solicit designations, such as "B-Corp Certification," to demonstrate their commitment to this principle. While doing good for good's sake is an ethical and moral imperative, there is a clear commercial benefit and advantages to pursuing a formal and visible CSR policy. And who would not want a competitive advantage?

According to a study by Cone Communications,[56] a solid majority of consumers support CSR in several ways:

- 63% of Americans are hopeful businesses will take the lead to drive social and environmental change moving forward, in the abdication of government regulations
- 78% want companies to address important social justice issues
- 87% will purchase a product because a company advocated for an issue they care about, and 76% will refuse to purchase a company's products or services upon learning it supported an issue contrary to their beliefs

You may be familiar with stories of how companies have integrated CSR into the fabric of their business culture. They take on many different activities to demonstrate this commitment[57]:

- Reducing carbon footprints
- Improving labor policies
- Participating in fair-trade
- Charitable giving
- Volunteering in the community
- Corporate policies that benefit the environment
- Socially and environmentally conscious investments

Companies like Cleveland Clinic, Eli Lilly, Cummins, and Best Buy earn a place on lists like the World's Most

Ethical Companies.[58] You might hear about companies, like Warby Parker or Bombas, that donate product to worthy causes based on product sales.

With public support at high levels, corporate social responsibility will continue to rise in importance to business strategies of all kinds. In marketing, its prominence will be felt across all channels, including sponsorship. For this reason, I use this chapter to unpack CSR and provide some guidance regarding its use in sponsorship.

The Opportunity to Stand Out

As you can tell by this point in *Sponsorship Strategy*, I've picked up many adages about marketing and business strategies over the years. Among my favorites is "when others turn right, we'll turn left." It is a saying that speaks to the importance of competitive differentiation and standing out in the crowd.

While a significant number of consumers support CSR, most sponsors do not leverage it. Only 26% of sponsors indicated that CSR is extremely important in their sponsorship decision making.[59] Frankly, it is surprising that sponsorships do not adopt CSR more regularly.

At many companies, the Board and C-suite still drive CSR decision making. In larger companies, the CSR function is expressed through a community relations or public relations team. Sponsorship, on the other hand, is driven by the marketing department. CSR implementation may not be part of this group's mandate. While good CSR initiatives can be seen in sponsorship, it is relegated to mere "good business" rather than a vital part of the sponsorship process.

However, at a time when it is not common for sponsorships to include a CSR component, sponsors that do can outshine those that do not. Regardless of its current level of acceptance, a much higher level of adoption will benefit sponsors by boosting visibility and favorability.

The Need for Visibility

Like any marketing platform, not all CSR-inspired initiatives have the same impact. First, CSR initiatives with high public visibility provide greater marketing impact than those less visible. "Causes that are highly visible in the public eye imply a greater likelihood of stakeholder awareness by means of media presence and publicity."[60] Similar to the factors that promote image transfer, the higher the visibility, the greater the impact of CSR in sponsorship.

For non-profits looking for sponsorship, visibility is even more important. It is not enough to be a non-profit with a worthy cause. There are thousands of worthy causes in the world. The non-profit also must have high visibility. Many times, sponsors will evaluate standard marketing KPIs to determine a non-profit's visibility: web traffic, social media followers, impressions from earned media, etc.

As someone who has been involved with many non-profits in my career, I recognize the internal management tension between allocating resources to fundraising versus marketing and public relations. Nevertheless, non-profits that want sponsorship opportunities must excel at marketing to be visible enough for potential sponsorship partners.

Second, the initiative must be promoted within the sponsorship in a way that gives it a high profile. Marketing practitioners certainly understand the importance of promotion. A PR mentor taught me "if people don't know it, you ain't done it." If you are going to promote a cause via sponsorship, promote it big time.

As is the case in other areas of sponsorship, a good idea alone does not produce powerful results. The combination of high visibility and proper promotion generate a positive impact for the sponsor. For this reason, CSR initiatives must be well conceived and executed.

CSR as a Sponsorship Turbo-Boost

Earlier in this book, I referenced the appeal of sponsorship over other marketing channels like advertising or direct marketing. Consumers perceive sponsorship as less in-your-face and thus, it is greeted with less resistance. An audience also appreciates the support that sponsors lend to events and the audience's enjoyment of them.

Sports, as a platform, also benefits from the fact that it is viewed as a content-neutral venue. It does not advocate (or at least it shouldn't) for a commercial, religious, or political agenda. The sports arena is a place where people from all walks of life and viewpoints can gather to drink too much, scream at the opposing team's players, and consume a 1,500-calorie snack. This is one reason that sports and sponsorship co-exist so nicely. Consumers view this pair as a relaxing respite from the thousands of overt sales messages they encounter daily.

When CSR is added to this mix, something amazing happens in the court of public opinion. Like the seemingly non-commercial sponsorship, CSR can "capitalize on the ubiquitous appeal of sport because it is regarded as a pure, non-political vehicle by which to send messages in a value-neutral mode and reach consumers and communities."[61]

When a neutral platform, like sports, is supported by non-commercial sponsorship and combined with the positives of CSR, the arrangement is "often perceived to as less commercially aggressive and faces less consumer resistance and skepticism, particularly when focusing on community-based properties or when relying on volunteer programmes (sic)."[62]

Not only is there less resistance and skepticism, there appears to be a greater benefit. At least one study argues that community relations-oriented sponsors provide a larger halo effect return than commercially oriented sponsorship.[63] There is a good opportunity for brands that can successfully combine their sponsorships (in sports and otherwise) with a CSR component. It is like driving a car with a turbo. It may be a fast already, but the turbo gives you even more power when you want it.

Three CSR Strategies in Sponsorship

CSR strategies can take many forms. Some involve youth development, health, and wellness, while others focus on economic opportunity or environmental sustainability. Sponsorships deploying CSR strategies generally take three forms: causes related to events, unrelated causes integrated into events, and sponsorship of a cause.

CAUSES RELATED TO EVENTS

In this category, the sponsor has determined that its CSR philosophy can be expressed as a logical extension of an existing event. The motivation is two-fold. The brand wants to support the event for the good of the audience, and it wants to contribute to a cause that does the audience some good.

Examples of this area include:

- Sponsor Credit Lyonnais promoting the use of bicycle helmets among children during the Tour de France.
- The NBA staging a charity tournament using the NBA 2K video game, with proceeds donated to the charity of the winner's choice to support COVID-19 relief efforts.

This strategy presents a relatively straightforward message to the consumer. The CSR goal flows organically from the event and is consistent with its purpose. In the Credit Lyonnais example, bike helmet use and the Tour de France go together like wine and cheese.

UNRELATED CAUSES INTEGRATED INTO EVENTS

In this category, the sponsors integrate an unrelated sponsor into an event. This may derive from a preexisting or long-standing relationship with the cause. Alternatively, the property may integrate its cause into the event for the same reason. Either way, there is high visibility of the cause, as well as community engagement and proximity.

Examples of this area include:

- Honda Canada featuring its work with Make-a-Wish Canada during the annual Honda Indy Toronto auto race. The CSR message is not about auto racing, but instead focuses on the important collaboration between Honda Canada and its charity partners.
- The NBA All-Star Game integrating local charities into its events, regardless of their connection to the sport.

In this strategy, the sponsor or property has some explaining to do. For instance, how does this CSR initiative align with the sponsor, property, or the event? The value of perceived sponsorship fit still applies in CSR-related programs, like its for-profit counterparts.

SPONSORSHIPS OF A CAUSE, WITH OR WITHOUT AN EVENT

This area involves sponsorship of a cause based on its contribution to socially beneficial goals. Hundreds, perhaps thousands, of worthy causes benefit from corporate sponsorship. I will take just a moment to differentiate between sponsorship and donation. Donation involves granting money without expectation of gain, whereas sponsorship generates advertising or a promotional benefit. Sponsors generally work quite hard to create promotional benefit aligned appropriately around a cause.

For example, sponsors of the Susan G. Komen Race for the Cure can message around the importance of breast cancer awareness and research. Ford has been a sponsor of this cause for decades, with its own Warriors in Pink apparel program, supporting Komen Affiliates. Likewise, Bank of America connects its support of Race for the Cure with the bank's Pink Ribbon Banking Affinity products and support for local volunteer events.

PNC Bank highlights the causes it sponsors on its corporate website. Thematically, it sponsors causes that "drive the success of our neighborhoods."[64] As part of its CSR policy, PNC highlights 15 causes in the arts, education, and economic development that help drive such success.

General Motors encourages charitable sponsorship proposals to be aligned around its commitment to STEM education, vehicle and road safety, and community development.[65] Boeing seeks partnerships that underscore its commitment to "positive change for our global communities."[66]

The Importance of Storytelling

Modest or humble brands find it harder to extract marketing benefit from CSR-related sponsorship. Under the rule of "if they don't know it, you ain't done it," every brand and property must incorporate robust integrated marketing communications into its CSR strategy. CSR has the potential to create highly emotional storytelling opportunities. As such, it is vital that the brand or the property dedicate bandwidth from their marketing and public relations resources to tell those stories.

Of course, such storytelling must be authentic, or it risks a consumer backlash. No one likes the company that contributes only for economic gain. But selfless businesses are revered. Take the example of a wireless phone company that introduces a don't-text-while driving campaign into its motorsports event sponsorship. The following tactics can contribute to the story-telling process:

- Communications that explain the reason underlying the CSR initiative. For example, a wireless phone company that has a no-texting-while-driving initiative at an event affirmatively communicates the death and injury toll from distracted drivers who text.
- Digital resources, available via event website or event social media, that describe alternatives to texting while driving.
- Integration of this CSR message into an experiential display at the motorsports event. Perhaps the consumer can participate in a racing simulator, but only after demonstrating that their mobile phone is in Do Not Disturb mode.
- Public service announcements during the event about

the dangers of texting while driving.
- Video testimonials running during the event that articulate the harm caused by this issue.

You get it. In addition to the reasons underlying the sponsorship, the CSR initiative of this hypothetical wireless services provider has been authentically communicated during the event. And, there are no lingering doubts that the consumer will understand the link between the sponsor and this CSR initiative.

The Future: CSR as FOMO

As I noted above, current trends suggest that CSR initiatives will be increasingly popular around the world. For this reason, such activities will become normalized as a mainstream element of sponsorship strategy.

From a brand's perspective, failing to adopt CSR may be seen as a type of "fear of missing out" (FOMO). Brands without a cause-related component to their sponsorship may even be seen as socially deficient. Thus, I expect to see tremendous growth in charitable sponsorship integrations.

Not only that, but brands will want properties to demonstrate CSR awareness and programs as a criterion of sponsorship. Properties without CSR initiatives will be at a competitive disadvantage to those that exhibit a robust commitment to their communities. Therefore, for properties seeking sponsorship, it will be important to understand the CSR commitment of each partner brand.

Event Social Responsibility

Properties will be expected to conform with certain CSR criteria, broadly described as "event social responsibility," or ESR. ESR refers to consumer expectations that an event "gives back to the communities in which it takes place."[67] Some of this pressure may come from audiences who value certain causes. It may also derive from brands that expect properties to act in a more socially responsible way.

Events that feature a CSR component enhance the potential value of a sponsorship.[68] Field research of consumer perceptions raises some interesting findings for sponsorship practitioners. First, as I discussed earlier, consumer reaction to "sponsor fit" is an important influence. Sponsor fit enhances the perception of the event and the sponsor when it comes to CSR. Second, when attendees identify with the event, they are more likely to view it as socially responsible. These attendees, in turn, also tend to patronize the companies that sponsor that event.

ESR research also speaks to the importance of sponsorship portfolio fit. Consumers are more likely to have positive impressions of an event and its sponsors when the entire line-up of sponsors makes sense. When attendees perceive a high degree of fit between the event and its sponsors, ESR benefit is intensified.

Finally, and most importantly, research indicates strong relationships between CSR, sponsorship, and word-of-mouth. When a consumer becomes a brand advocate by spreading the word about a product or service, the marketer has hit a home run.[69] This would also be the marketer's brand objective when engaging in sponsorship. Research findings also conclude that alignment of sponsorship portfolio fit and ESR bolsters event word-of-mouth.[70] Wouldn't you be more likely to talk up an event and sponsors who supported a cause close to your heart? Of course, you would.

Practical Impacts

As an authentic and important form of expression, CSR is ideal for sponsorship. In the future, executive leadership will require CSR as integral, just as signage or event activation are part and parcel of event sponsorships now.

Additionally, brands will incorporate their own causes into sponsorship. Charities and corporate values will be expressed before, during, and after events. If properties do not have pre-existing CSR initiatives and policies, they will be at a competitive disadvantage to those that do.

At the same time, brands will scrutinize events to determine if they pass a minimum threshold of CSR compatibility. I would not be surprised to see the following checklist on a brand manager's sponsorship clipboard:

- ✓ Does the property have a sustainability plan and goal towards carbon-neutral events?
- ✓ Does the property have its own CSR policy towards its community?
- ✓ Does the property contribute to the economic

development of its community?
- ✓ Does the property integrate local charities into its facility and events all year round?
- ✓ What is the CSR policy of the other sponsors in the property's sponsorship portfolio?
- ✓ How can the property's communications channels amplify the sponsor's CSR messages and policies?
- ✓ What opportunities exist to engage the property's community before and after the event with a CSR message?

A progressive and smart property will already have answers to all these questions and more. In fact, properties that lead the way with authentic and sustainable commitments can use this area as a competitive differentiator. I am not talking about a sports franchise that sends its athletes out to local food pantries on Thanksgiving weekend. I mean truly committed properties that consistently make a difference in their communities.

Can sponsorship be a force for good? Of course, it can. Like any other marketing tool, it has resonance as a storytelling mechanism. It can raise hopes. It can create awareness. It can focus attention on the things that need it.

CHAPTER 8

THE PIONEER STRATEGY

About 800 climbers attempt to scale Mount Everest annually. Most of us could not name one of the climbers. However, many know the names of Sir Edmund Hillary and Tenzing Norgay, the climbers who, in 1953, were the first to reach the peak of the tallest mountain on Earth.

In the 19th century, California experienced a gold rush. Prospectors, braving physical danger, raced to stake their claims. The first to find gold on their land were winners.

First movers often receive recognition and success. That is why so much attention is given to "first mover advantage" in business strategy. First-mover theory is when "a product or service gains a competitive advantage by being the first to market with a product or service."[71] First movers can have a tremendous advantage – just look at companies like Amazon, Apple, or Google.

The benefits to first movers are substantial when it comes to brand recognition and customer loyalty.[72] This makes sense. When you are the oasis in the middle of the desert, you will be remembered by every parched traveler who partakes of a sip of water. Other potential benefits include the ability to control scarce strategic resources and making it too costly for buyers to switch to the competitive products of second movers.[73]

Of course, while there are advantages to be the first-moving pioneer in a market, there can be downsides as well. For instance, first movers make mistakes, which can be costly. The operating costs in a market may be lower later. Also, the second and third movers identify areas for improvement that the first mover overlooked.[74] Myspace preceded Facebook, and it is obvious how that ended.

At this point, you might ask, "how does this apply to sponsorship?" That is a good question that I have been struggling with for most of my sponsorship career. There is a reason for that.

I was trained as an attorney. As you may know, attorneys are trained in risk mitigation. To say the legal profession is risk averse would be an understatement. For this reason, early in my sponsorship career, I advised brands to steer clear of new events or new properties. Why? There are too many unknowns. Would the event have decent attendance? Do promoters know what they are doing? Would unforeseen circumstances create brand risk? With no track record, all I could see was the potential for failure.

Although many brand managers are not attorneys, many view risk the same way – especially at larger companies. Risk is to be avoided at all costs. As the adage goes, "no one ever got fired for hiring IBM." Similarly, a sponsorship manager would rarely be rebuked for taking a risk on long-time marquis sports properties like the NFL or NBA.

However, to the victor go the spoils. The brand that takes a knee-jerk approach to sponsorship risk will never know the success that this strategy can bring. As braver brands have discovered, there is substantial benefit, if it can be found.

Furthermore, second, third, or fourth mover brands must fight an uphill battle. The first mover received brand recognition as a result of its bold move. But the second mover arrives into an environment a bit more cluttered, a little more prone to brand confusion and with consumer loyalty more staked out.

Adopting a pioneer strategy can be an effective way of creating strong sponsorship impact. Now, I'll explore how to be a sponsor pioneer – in relative safety.

First Movers with Properties

A brand can be a first mover with a new property. In an age of innovation, there are a variety of new properties available for sponsorship. Sponsors either find a new property that has emerged, or the brand creates the property from its imagination and creativity.

NEW AND EMERGING EVENTS

At the time of the writing of this book, there are several new property examples to point to. For instance, sponsorship practitioners are hearing more and more about sports like foot golf, pickleball, or quidditch from *Harry Potter* fame. However, the king of emerging sports at present is esports.

Admittedly, many of us are late to the esports boom compared to esports purists. Although I am a life-long video game player, esports as a "thing" escaped my notice as a marketer until my then 16-year-old son asked me to take him to an MLG Major Event of CS-GO in Columbus, Ohio. The Nationwide Arena was filled to near-capacity. I was astounded. More like, I was surprised by what I did not see.

Aside from a pallet of Monster Energy drink in the middle of the atrium, I did not see sponsorship. I did not see hospitality. I did not see team or player merchandise. It was crazy to see such a huge audience with no brands speaking to them.

When I got back to my agency, I began to make phone calls to friends and colleagues who represent or work with brands. What did they think of the esports? Some of them knew its power. Some of them even had even dipped their toes in the water. However, for the most part, I received this answer most often: "Yes. It is on our radar. But we are not sure if it has legs. Besides, there is a lot of concern about the violence in first-person shooter games." Here is that risk factor rearing its ugly head. A wait-and-see strategy. A typical response for large brands with risk-averse corporate cultures.

However, endemics in the esports world thought otherwise. Intel was chief among them. Intel could certainly be described as an esports pioneer. Its high-profile association with the sport dates back to 2006 with title sponsorship of *Intel Extreme Masters*. While their relationship with esports made sense from a brand and product perspective – sponsorships promoted the sale of gaming PCs run on powerful Intel chips – it still required courage to be a first mover in an emerging market.

THE BESPOKE PROPERTY

A team of marketing strategists, including Christopher Lochhead, first proposed the business strategy called "category design."[75] Category design describes companies that create, develop, and dominate new categories of products and services. Rather than fight off competitors in a category, companies like Uber or Airbnb created their own category, developed a market around it, and then dominated the category.

I love this strategy. It is ideal for sponsorship marketers who understand their brands and know how to cross-validate their brand with culture. Rather than seeking properties that happen to align with their brand values, they create properties to promote them.

1. Music:

Harman International's JBL Speakers division was looking for a brand immersion opportunity to bring together its sponsored celebrities. It created JBL Fest in Las

Vegas to serve as a three-day living sponsorship filled with concerts, parties, and celebrity appearances. It could have been any concert or party in Las Vegas. Instead, it was a living brand sponsorship for JBL that drove engagement for consumers, customers, employees, and vendors.

2. Extreme Sports:

Writing a book about sponsorship strategy would be incomplete without mentioning the 800-pound gorilla in the extreme sports category: Red Bull. Red Bull brilliantly created properties that perfectly align with its brand values. In categories from auto races to air races to cliff diving, Red Bull gives you wings. Perhaps my favorite is their Red Bull Flugtag event. In Flugtag, entrants fly human-powered, homemade flying machines off piers into lakes or oceans. This holy cow moment certainly embodies the extreme notion that Red Bull "gives you wings."

First Movers in Categories

First movers in a category generally arise through the introduction of new product or the advent of a new technology. In the new product category, CBD products have experienced growing popularity (and legality). CBD products are being legalized on a state-by-state basis, and the UFC has entered into a sponsorship relationship with a CBD company.

Similarly, with the U.S. Supreme Court ruling against

federal prohibition on sports gambling, certain states have legalized this activity. Sports organizations have followed suit by aligning sponsorship relationships with sports book organizations like MGM and William Hill or mobile gaming platforms like Draft Kings and Fan Duel.

The Prudent Pioneer's Checklist

My family has been vacationing in the Outer Banks of North Carolina for years. Each year we return, we are reminded of the story of Lost Colony of Roanoke. In 1587, a group of English settlers, the first real European pioneers in what would become the United States, arrived on the North Carolina coast. No one knows how or why, but in 1590, the entire colony disappeared without a trace. To this day, the colony's disappearance remains a mystery.

Pioneer strategies can yield substantial rewards. However, the story of the Lost Colony reminds us that with big rewards comes significant risk. Based on sponsorship successes and failure in the past, I hope the following considerations can help you establish a successful strategy:

THE PROPERTY OR CATEGORY HAS EXPERIENCED LEADERSHIP AND MANAGEMENT THAT IS RESPONSIVE TO SPONSORSHIP NEEDS.

Almost by definition new properties and categories are the province of entrepreneurs. Entrepreneurs excel in many areas. They exhibit passion, fearlessness, and tenacity.

Depending on the individuals involved, they may or may not be good managers. And, even if they are good managers, they may not be good leaders. Even if they are good at both, they may not have the requisite experience to successfully navigate the shark-infested waters of a new market. There is a reason why 30% of businesses fail within the first two years of opening.[76]

When thinking about this issue in the world of sports, the lesson of mixed martial arts (MMA) comes to mind. In the 1990s, the sports market witnessed a resurgence of this ancient combat sport. However, certain promotions had rules that allowed or even encouraged extreme brutality. What sponsor would want to enter the octagon under these circumstances, even when tempted by an attractive audience base? Answer: not many.

However, once the UFC entered the market, the dynamics of MMA began to change: rule changes eliminating capricious brutality; professional management focused on brand-building and event promotion. In short, it was an experienced team of sports executives and managers who created a billion-dollar dynamo worthy of sponsorship investment.

New properties may also employ a team unskilled in sponsor care and feeding. For example, they may not have experience collecting data about sponsorship results or they have not learned the art of asset fulfillment. In these circumstances, the risk may be too high. Even with a new property that performs well with its audience, the sponsor may not receive the benefit of the bargain in terms of the property's obligations to the sponsor.

THE BRAND RETAINS AN EXPERT WHO HAS SUBJECT-MATTER KNOWLEDGE OF THE CATEGORY

In the mid-19th century, thousands of pioneers died while traveling the treacherous Oregon Trail from Nebraska to Oregon. The survivors credit the skill of trail guides who helped wagon trains find the right direction or showed travelers how to prevent deadly cholera.

During my career in auto racing, I saw many successful millionaires and billionaires enter the sport as team owners or sponsors. Filled with the same confidence that fueled their success in non-motorsports businesses, these new entrants had no idea about the eccentricities of racing business practices, the unique values of racing fans, or subtle best-practices related to past successes and failures. Often times, the over-confident and under-advised left racing unsuccessfully, well before they could establish subject-matter expertise.

There are sponsorship managers whose careers ended up careening off the marketing cliff for lack of expert knowledge in a new category. Envy Gaming's Mark Coughlin notes that experts can help you mitigate unnecessary expense or identify hard-to-see opportunities.

THE PRODUCT ITSELF IS NOT PRONE TO UNKNOWNS.

It is one thing to be a pioneer in a new category or property. It is quite another to be plopped down in the middle of a product experiment. There are risks, and then there are unnecessary risks.

Take, for example, esports. The risk of the product is relatively low. Video games have been around since the late 1970s. The product itself is fairly stable. While there are risks associated with promotion and production, they can be managed by vetting a promoter's technical skills. Does that person know the way around a stage and LAN server, for example? Historically, there have been a few issues with match fixing. However, overall, a product like this is not prone to unknowns.

But there are other products and categories where this is not the case. Specifically, vaping and CBD products come to mind. It is not my intention to rain on anyone's parade. However, health concerns may present challenges to faithfully sponsoring these products. At its onset, there were many properties eager to take the money of new e-cigarette companies with marketing money to burn. However, now those properties on the vaping bandwagon have concerns as child marketing issues and unexplained lung injuries started making the news.

CBD is another market that looks great right now but may pose risks down the road. According to the U.S. Food & Drug Administration, it has only seen "limited data about CBD safety and these data point to real risks that need to be considered before taking CBD for any reason."[77] While some properties were first movers in this category, there may be an unknown quantum of downstream brand risk associated with it in the long term.

THE AUDIENCE IS CLEARLY DEFINED,
EVEN IF IT IS NOT LARGE.

If the new property or category understands its audience, it is likely that the audience is defined at some level. When Red Bull rolls out a new event or series, it has a keen understanding of its audience on both the product level and from its extreme sports experience.

Also, it is not necessary for early pioneers to have the throw-weight of a 150,000 attendee NASCAR race. If the audience is dialed in and loyal, the sponsor is building loyalty one attendee at a time.

One word, though, about shifting audiences. In a new property, the practitioner should continue to measure the composition of its audience over time. When Facebook first launched, Mark Zuckerberg wanted to digitize the online directory of Harvard students so men and women could see one another – ostensibly for the purposes of dating. From that original college-student audience, Facebook has evolved into the "social media used by your parents." I am not denigrating Facebook; simply making the point that audience profiles evolve.

THE PROPERTY CREATES AN UPSIDE
FOR BEING THE FIRST MOVER

There is a flipside to be the first-mover or pioneer in a category or property. Such parties are relatively desperate for a sponsorship partner. Anyone who has sold sponsorship as a new property understands that the brand community is usually pretty skeptical. This is a result of the risk that I described above. Thus, sales in the beginning is an uphill battle.

From the brand's perspective, the greater the risk, the greater the potential reward. First-movers should expect to be rewarded down the road. Sure, there is reward of a good sponsorship relationship. If the audience is properly identified and the property is successful, the sponsor will benefit. However, there also should be a bit of protection. After all, you would not want to be the founding sponsor of a property only to be told to hit the road once the property hits the big time.

In this circumstance, the brand should consider a few contractual safeguards to protect its long-term benefits without locking in long-term risk. For example, brands can ask for category exclusivity in the short term to keep out pesky competitors. In the long term, brands can consider options to renew, first rights of refusal, or first rights of negotiation. Whichever strategy the business team and its legal counsel chooses, there should be a way to protect gold earned during the initial gold rush.

THE STRATEGIST'S TOOLBOX

CHAPTER 9

STRATEGY WITHIN CONTRACT TERMS

Many sponsorship practitioners know their way around a contract. So often, the sponsorship agreement may be the only place where all the terms exist. But this is not a book on legal practice, and I am not offering legal advice. Instead, I want to note the many places where legal concepts and strategy intersect. A working knowledge of these relationships enables sponsorship practitioners to craft effective strategies. Additionally, foreknowledge of these issues helps business professionals decide key issues before their attorneys become involved.

Exclusivity

Exclusivity is a special beast within sponsorship. From a marketing perspective, it creates an advantage for a brand that traditional advertising cannot always match. If you watch NFL football on Sunday afternoon television, you are likely to see commercials from multiple auto manufacturers.

However, if you attend the game live, there may be only one official car of your favorite team. This exclusivity grants the recipient a special advantage; it is the most valuable benefit of sponsorship.[78]

Mark Coughlin, who represented wireless carrier Sprint in its title sponsor relationship with NASCAR, credited category exclusivity with incredible ROI in new account generation. It is interesting to note that Coughlin also sees benefit for a sponsor in a non-exclusive sponsorship environment. In circumstances where competitor-sponsors are activating sponsorships side-by-side, which is typical in auto racing, brands work harder to achieve results. Just like in the marketplace where they compete, some of these results are better than had they been attained in an exclusive environment. Additionally, a sponsor will pay a premium for exclusivity. Unless they can achieve the results, which were better than a non-exclusive environment, that additional expense may not be worth it.

Some of biggest battles in sponsorship administration involve the protection (or near infringement) of exclusivity rights. From a strategy perspective, there are three aspects to exclusivity to consider in the sponsorship planning process: shared exclusivity rights, ambushes, and previous sponsors.

SHARED EXCLUSIVITY

When a property has strong leverage at the negotiating table, it will inevitability seek to squeeze more similar sponsors into its stable of categories. For instance, property A may sell a single exclusive category – like carbonated beverages. However, the more attractive property B may sell categories in carbonated beverages, juices, and water. I see this in a variety of areas, including beverages, automobiles (luxury vs consumer), and health care (official health system vs official orthopedic solution).

These are great from a property perspective. More money, more money, more money! Brands should be leery, though. Often, I see brands rationalize shared exclusivity arrangements as the price of admission to align with a hot property. However, the prospect for brand dilution and weak association values is real. Often, the sponsors sharing exclusivity are competitors in grocery stores or on Amazon. Therefore, I recommend surveying during the sponsorship to determine if the brand has indeed generated increased awareness, improved opinion, or increased purchase consideration.

AMBUSH

When one brand has exclusivity, its market competitors cannot leverage the property. Sometimes, these competitors still try to associate their brands with the already-taken property. This is known as ambush marketing.

Without exclusivity, there would be no ambush. Ambush strategies abound, both cute and brazen. If you are the ambusher, be sure to have your attorney on speed dial. I have witnessed many ways ambushers walk up to the line of infringement.

An ambushing brand may buy a billboard outside the arena. It may buy general admission tickets for its sample-bearing street team and send them into the stadium. Some ambushers replace the event name with a generic name in advertising running contemporaneously with an event or even on the event broadcast itself. How many times have you seen advertisements urging fans to buy their product before the "Big Game," the week before the Super Bowl?

The exclusive sponsor should incorporate anti-ambush strategies in its pre-event meetings with its property partner. First, the sponsor should never be in the position to need to enforce its rights. The property should protect the sponsor's exclusive relationship. As such, sponsors should confirm with the property ahead of time what its anti-infringement plan looks like.

Second, for major events, the sponsor should confirm the existence of "clean zones," or areas outside a sponsored event venue that the property protects from the products or services of competing sponsors.

Third, for televised events, the sponsor's media buyers should keep tabs on spots that competitors may have purchased. Reviewing ads after an event will not protect the sponsor's rights in a given event year. But, in the case of multi-year agreements, the sponsor and its property partner can prepare for future ambushes and infringements.

THE PREDECESSOR

If an event is not new, a just-arriving sponsor may have to deal with a competitor who previously held the exclusive partner slot. If that predecessor sponsor has a long history with the property, it surely has built strong brand equity with fans and consumers. For years after R.J Reynolds Tobacco Company left auto racing following its 30-year run, some NASCAR fans continued to refer to its elite series as "Winston Cup," even as Nextel took over the exclusive title sponsorship.

Other times, the predecessor does not even go away. For example, a sponsor may vacate the official sponsor slot of a national sports league to a competitor. But instead of leaving the scene, the predecessor sponsor continues to heavily advertise on television during the league's games. It no longer has the "official sponsor of XYZ League" moniker. However, the reach and frequency of its advertisements continue to create the association between that sport and the brand.

If you are the successor brand sponsor, you should consider if the strength of the predecessor brand and its "residual brand equity"[79] have diminished the value of the early years of your sponsorship. In these circumstances, the brand may consider paying a lower price than its predecessor early on as a result of needing to spend more on leverage and activation to build its new brand equity.

As the successor brand, you also should have a counterstrategy in place to address encroaching predecessors. If the previous brand does not infringe on the technical rights of the successor, there is no legal strategy to employ. However, you should pay special vigilance in several areas.

First, if the property is televised, be ready to go toe-to-toe with enough commercial spots to at least match the brand association of the predecessor. Second, in those commercial spots, the successor should consider custom sponsorship advertising creatively tagged with the "official sponsor of XYZ League" logo or word mark. Third, the successor should ask the property to monitor adjacent areas around the venue for infringing activity. Fourth, the successor should monitor the predecessor if it tries to pick off "ancillary properties." For example, if the brand is a league sponsor, the predecessor may try to pick off teams, venues, or athletes. Note this problem not only exists among predecessors but competitors across multi-level sponsorships like leagues or national federations.

Term (Duration) of the Relationship

Most sponsorship veterans believe that the duration of a sponsorship relationship should be "the longer the better." It is true that it takes time to hit one's stride in maximizing sponsorship value. Regardless of the degree of planning or the experience of the brand's sponsorship team, the rookie year of a sponsorship is a time of trial-and-error and learning. "Why was my product display in the less-trafficked area?" "What could I have done better in the PR lead-up to the event?" During this time, strategy and tactics are tuned up.

Another reason for wanting longer terms involves brainstorming. It takes time for the brand and property to work together and develop trust and friendships. When people who trust one another work together long enough, a funny thing happens. They start to generate creative ideas, and strategies can take a new direction. A direction that can improve the sponsor's return on investment. In a short-term relationship, there simply is not time for this brainstorming magic to occur.

However, I was struck by a recent sponsor survey that indicated how a whopping 58% of sponsors said they were looking to drop at least one sponsorship *prior* to its renewal.[80] The agency conducting the survey surmised that dissatisfaction may have stemmed from the property failing to keep up with changing priorities and benefits. For example, the property may be more concerned with onsite signage, while the brand is concerned with social media.[81]

From a strategy perspective, I recommend two approaches to the issue of term. First, while a longer term may be in both parties' interest, the sponsor may want to consider adding contract benchmarks to its agreement. If certain benchmarks are not met prior to its expiration, the sponsor may elect an early termination.

Second, flexibility is key. Either the sponsor gauges whether the property is flexible, or the parties agree to substitute different inventory categories during the term of the agreement. In my experience, it is in the property's interest to remain flexible during the contract term. It is one of the most appreciated aspects of the sponsorship relationship in the eyes of many brands.

A First-Year Event

Should a brand agree to sponsor a first-year event? I am of two minds on this subject.

On the "yes" side, there is the first-mover or pioneer advantage, as I've discussed previously. It can be advantageous if a brand blazes a trail with a new event and captures all the attention for itself at the expense of its competitors.

On the "no" side, there is shouldering all the risk of a new promoter, a new event, a somewhat unknown audience, and no track record. Generally, most brands are not willing to take a lot of risk, unless it is with a familiar or well-known promoter.

From a contract perspective, if you decide to sponsor a first-year event, try to hedge your downside risk in two ways. First, create milestones that the promoter must reach prior to the event. This may involve the number of tickets sold, marketing dollars spent, or media campaigns placed. If the property blows the milestone, make it a terminable event for your sponsorship.

Second, structure the lion's share of your sponsorship fee to be paid as close to the event as possible – or even after the event. This mitigates risk from unscrupulous promoters or failed events that do not even answer the bell.

Incentives

Business agreements frequently include some type of incentives provision. Incentives for early payment or completion are a few examples. In the world of sponsorships, sports sponsorship giant Anheuser-Busch InBev has made its incentives policy widely known as a potential contract provision.

In AB InBev's pay-for-performance model, a property is paid a base compensation. However, in a negotiated range of metrics within the control of the property, AB InBev agrees to increase its investment with the property if certain thresholds are reached on or off the field. For instance, "a playoff appearance or boost in attendance could lead to more sponsor money from AB InBev. A new digital platform that engages fans or increases awareness of AB InBev brands might spur larger payouts."[82]

According to Nick Kelly, U.S. marketing head for Anheuser-Busch InBev, properties prefer incentives related to social and digital media.[83] However, incentives can be as creative as the negotiating parties' imaginations. Nevertheless, imagination needs to be tempered by reality. In general, I would recommend the following criteria in establishing sponsorship incentives.

- Choose a metric that is fairly within the property's control. Social media performance might be fair. Good weather events not so much.
- Select a metric that is reasonably verifiable. In some

industries, actual attendance figures are a subject of (ahem) creativity on the property's part. If such a metric is selected, a brand may wish to have verification or audit rights. However, it is easier to select a metric that comes from some reliable third-party service.

- Use incentives with a property you trust and with whom have an ongoing relationship. Some less-principled properties cut corners or bend the rules to hit their incentive numbers. This defeats the purpose of the incentive.
- Express the metric as clearly and succinctly as possible. This avoids disagreements years after the incentive was written.
- Choose a reward other than money. It is easy for a brand to write a check. However, there may be rewards or investments beyond cash value. For instance, a brand may choose to increase its media investment or add another promotional campaign supporting a sponsored event. The potential windfall to the property, in some cases, would exceed a cash incentive.

Beware of Technology

Later in this book, I reference the opportunities and challenges that new technology presents. In this chapter related to the strategy of sponsorship terms, I wanted to note a few items, particularly in the category of challenges. Because technology changes so quickly, and regulatory bodies are adapting their standards to catch up, I always recommend consulting legal counsel on any of these issues:

DISPLAY RIGHTS

In the days of static signage, it was simple to describe the image rights that a sponsor could exploit in venue. However, with increasingly flexible in-stadium LED signage, including video screens, ribbon boards and the like, sponsors should be wary of over-detailed display rights in contract language. One attorney, experienced in this field, recommends that the parties use flexible language as well as a "clear process for the parties to agree how [a] new technology could be used."[84]

VIRTUAL REALITY

Virtual reality enables properties and sponsors to create an alternative reality for commercial rights. Technology can transport an event attendee to a virtual world filled with sponsor signage, property trade dress, and a new world of conflicts.

SOCIAL MEDIA AND USER-GENERATED CONTENT

Every property and sponsor want to use social media and event apps to amplify the impact of a sponsorship. However, properties may want to limit the frequency of social media posting or the type of content used via social media because of the implementation burden.

Similarly, social media users do not necessarily relinquish their rights to names/images/likenesses. They may object to being used in a commercial promotion. For this reason, attorneys may recommend that sponsors and properties align with certain third-party platform providers like Snap, Inc., which provides legal cover for its partners in this regard. In the case of SnapChat, its Terms of Service automatically establishes a royalty-free license to use user generated content, transferable to Snap's business partners.[85]

Access to Measurement and Audience

Properties can be important sources of measurement information about the effectiveness of a sponsorship. Often, properties commission surveys on-site to measure a variety of event or sponsorship issues. In the contract, it would be advisable to request coordination or data sharing on these measurements.

Similarly, if the property does not survey, then the brand could seek permission in the contract to survey the property's audience. Such a survey involves on-site access for the brand's surveyors. Additionally, if an online survey is conducted, the brand should secure the rights and assistance from the property to reach out to the property's audience by email.

Finally, the property's audience can offer keen insights or opportunities to the sponsor. Because a shared target audience is necessary for successful sponsorships, the property's audience is, by definition, a target-rich environment of current and prospective customers. Access to this audience, through email marketing lists or lists of addresses, can be valuable for the sponsor. These should be obtained through a contract and adhere to all data-sharing laws and regulations.

The Marketing Guarantee

In some sponsorship relationships, a property may require a sponsor to commit to a marketing guarantee. A marketing guarantee is the minimum amount a sponsor will spend on certain leverage activities. These activities may include television advertisements, on-site activation, or digital projects.

Whether the property can persuade the sponsor to commit to a marketing guarantee is a matter of bargaining power. In my experience, marketing guarantees are prevalent when properties need to ensure advertising revenue to television broadcast partners. For example, if ESPN was going to pay a property a hefty rights fee to broadcast a certain set of events, it wanted to minimize the risk that the properties' partners would not advertise on the ESPN broadcast.

Although many brands consider marketing guarantees onerous, there are good justifications for using them. Professionally, I think the marketing guarantee conversation is useful because it forces both parties to think about leverage of the sponsorship relationship. It also differentiates prepared sponsors from the unprepared.

CHAPTER 10

TECHNOLOGY IMPACTING SPONSORSHIP STRATEGY

Technology has changed the way we live. Gen X remembers their college days when they ordered pizza on corded phones and used typewriters for their term papers. The Gen Z children of that generation are digital natives who grew up with smartphones. Within two generations, technology has changed life profoundly.

It has also changed marketing and sponsorship. Sponsorship professionals must be as adept at social media, digital marketing, and software applications as they are at defining inventory and structuring relationships. With the breakneck pace of innovation, I would not want *Sponsorship Strategy* to date itself by referencing technology that will change before the ink is dry on this book's first edition. For this reason, this chapter is meant to be a reminder to monitor technology change closely and not as a primer on today's most-utilized tools. Versatility and flexibility are key to keeping your sponsorships relevant.

There are many ways for sponsorship practitioners to stay tech savvy. I recommend several practices to our clients:

1. Read trade publications and thought leadership sources like *WIRED, Recode, Fast Company* or *Innovation & Tech Today.*

2. Identify your friends and colleagues who are early adopters. A dozen years ago, I found the Apple iPhone through one such friend who called my then-current phone "my grandfather's mobile phone."

3. Attend trade shows like the Consumer Electronics Show where exhibitors like to represent the cutting-edge.

4. Challenge your staff periodically to bring one new tech idea to team meetings.

5. Stay multi-generational. Different age groups use technology differently. Understanding generational trends increase your sponsorship's relevancy.

6. Grab a new technology and experiment. I definitely recommend this technique to colleagues who do not understand esports. A few days with an Xbox will cure that gap in their knowledgebase.

Technology has impacted sponsorship by empowering brands and properties with more tools, keener insights, and extended reach. I will unpack each area to help you better understand how to craft new and more effective strategies.

More Tools

For many years, physical signage was the primary way that sponsors spoke to their audiences. Even today, when the general public thinks of sponsorship, the sponsor's sign on the ballpark's outfield fence comes to mind. But now there are so many new tools that enable sponsors to speak to audiences, including virtual reality, social media, streaming, and in-arena technology.

VIRTUAL REALITY

Virtual reality (VR) has many applications within and outside the marketing profession. That is why the market continues to expand exponentially. What was a $7.3 billion market globally in 2018 is anticipated to reach $120.5 billion in 2026.

I mentioned virtual reality (VR) in *Chapter 9* because its use has legal implications for sponsorships. As a sponsorship tool, its impact will be a game changer. VR has already started to change the way we see, buy, and structure sponsorships.

From the seller's perspective, VR can be used as a sales tool, as a sponsorship service tool, an activation tool, and as a new sponsorship category.[86] As a sales tool, VR gives life to a non-existent sponsorship asset. For example, the use of VR to help sell new stadium suites or naming rights is potent. The power to visualize a new sponsorship opportunity before it is constructed improves the prospects for sales success. This tool wields immense power because in the event business, there is no substitute for being present – even in a virtual sense.

Similarly, using VR to service a sponsor can be equally powerful. It is one thing to receive a PowerPoint deck with your signage locations noted in two-dimensional photos. It is quite another to be virtually transported to the event to see your signage exactly as attendees would see it.

At events, VR can be used as an activation tool by virtually transporting attendees to worlds filled with brand-inspired messages. What was once considered a toy or novelty has elevated to an experiential tool that enhances the event experience.

VR as a new category has great strategic potential. Like video game advertising where the players of *Rocket League* experience a Hot Wheels integration in-game,[87] VR could potentially create an alternate universe of categories. In the real world, an event may have ten category sponsors. It is conceivable that the VR execution of that same event would have ten *different* category sponsors. For now, it seems that VR categories simply extend the on-site experience. For example, Samsung's arrangement with Six Flags Entertainment created a VR sponsorship category that augmented the physical experience with the parks' coasters as well as extended the experience with new virtual coasters.[88] However, I expect VR to create fascinating conversations between brands and properties, with heated discussions between their attorneys as ownership rights are sorted out.

SOCIAL MEDIA

Not that long ago, sponsors considered social media "nice" add-ons to integrated marketing campaigns. Today is a different story. Social media platforms, like Twitter and Facebook, are huge billion-person platforms that offer access to every corner of the globe. What was once an add-on is now a pivotal part of a sponsorship technology strategy. In fact, social media are the most used channels to activate sponsorships.[89]

Mainstream social media expand opportunities for brands to engage with their audiences. However, social media should be considered more than a static message delivery system. Sponsors have the potential to connect with each property's social community and establish personal connections – especially among audiences it may not have spoken to directly before.

VIDEO AND LIVE STREAMING

Like the other technologies referenced in this chapter, video and live streaming have changed the game for sponsors. Video content can be easily captured via smartphone or "pro-sumer" cameras. Polished video content is distributed via social media, including video platforms like YouTube. With increasing data transmission capabilities, live streaming events and experiences has become commonplace.

From a strategy perspective, video and live streaming offer three opportunities for sponsorships. First, properties have the opportunity to partner with traditional broadcasters to offer over-the-top (OTT) content offerings. These offerings may be the event itself or a behind-the-scenes opportunity.

Second, brands get the chance to create novel content, which leverages their rights to use property intellectual property. This can be done as value-added content for audiences. Alternatively, content could integrate various other sponsorship elements such as corporate social responsibility or cause marketing.

Third, brands and properties can facilitate the creation of user-generated video content. Authentic video showing fans enjoying an activity, courtesy of the property and its sponsor, benefits the sponsorship.

IN-ARENA TECHNOLOGY

Tech advances in sponsorship often appear in stadiums and arenas first. At least, they are *noticed* there first. This is ironic because tech in stadiums has a relatively high barrier to entry: capital improvements are expensive. Nonetheless, fans noticed when displays evolved from incandescent bulbs to LED scoreboards to digital displays. Then, ribbon displays began to ring arenas. With advances, sponsorship messaging opportunities increased many-fold.

In-arena Wi-Fi now connects attendee smartphones with specialty apps delivering customized messages about sponsors. Additionally, these interactions create longer-term relationships as fans part with their email addresses and mobile numbers in exchange for access to the property's content or services.

However, stadium technology will continue to advance to make the in-event experience safer, more hygienic, and more convenient. For instance, properties are partnering with companies, like Clear, to leverage biometrics and identity verification technology to control access to events or verify ages for beer purchases.

All of these technologies offer new interception points, where sponsors can find and target audiences.

More Insights

Technology offers sponsors and properties the ability to learn valuable insights about their audiences. Ever since the term "cookie" entered our lexicon, companies have been able to track the way customers use technology and what that use says about them. In order to comprehensively understand audiences, collaborating brands and properties can integrate disparate sources of insight data from digital media, smartphone apps, RFID technology, and a variety of survey platforms.

DIGITAL MEDIA

When an audience interacts with digital media, it creates a profile of demographic and psychographic information for sponsors and properties.

From web interactions, Google Analytics offers a wealth of information on audience demographics, as well the interests and behaviors of website visitors. Affinity categories can demonstrate whether a property's website attracts home-and-garden enthusiasts or fitness buffs.

Larger social media platforms also offer free audience analysis tools. Twitter Analytics and Facebook Audience Insights both provide a wealth of data about audience demographics, interests, and buying styles. Insights about gender, age, and location can be used to cross reference other demographic sources. Imagine the power in the sponsorship sales process if a property can demonstrate that its audience is actively looking for the prospect brand's products.

From email newsletters, most email distribution platforms enable the sender to analyze which audience members are interacting with various types of content. These data points enable users the ability to build interest profiles, which can then be leveraged by sponsors.

Smartphone apps offer another opportunity to accumulate digital breadcrumbs. Many properties offer smartphone apps to enhance the fan experience. Depending on the app and the property, the technology can track scores, order food, find parking, or play videos. In all circumstances, the property can track which content the audience considers valuable to better understand how to use it.

FAN ENGAGEMENT

Technology has helped properties and brands better understand fan engagement. For example, radio-frequency identification (RFID) technology has helped upgrade the event experience. When users register an RFID tag, provided at an event, the user can then access nearby sponsored experiences. Post-event, the property and an experience sponsor can analyze the manner and frequency of fan engagement.

In the area of fan engagement, technology advancements in surveys offer new and varied insights for brands and properties. Traditional survey opportunities, like on-site intercepts and panel surveys, are still helpful for brand awareness or image. However, the advent of technologies, like Survey Monkey, have put surveying in the hands of nearly everyone.

While the ability to build surveys has improved, so has user experience in taking them. Today, you will see iPad survey opportunities everywhere, including each event activation. These, combined with web and smartphone surveys, provide many new opportunities to generate fan engagement insights.

Extended Reach

Technology has demolished the idea that sponsorships should be territorial. This is particularly true in the area of event sponsorships.

Twenty years ago, sponsors and properties developed strategies to capitalize on a geographic region around a particular event; events were defined as local, regional, national, or global. Television broadcasting and distribution, along with syndicated radio, defined the outer edge of geographic reach.

Today, with the right resources and a clever strategy, a local event could have international reach. VR and live streaming can accommodate audience members thousands of miles of away. A fan app provides statistical insights that are sometimes more valuable than available to live attendance. And a strong social media presence helps the community feel like they are actually attending.

Strategically, properties and sponsors should consider how they can leverage technology to boost sponsorship by minimizing dated geographical constraints. In the following chapter, I will discuss how this new paradigm of "non-geographic" thinking can help sponsors reach avid fans far from an event, boost image transfer, and create "off-site resonance."

CHAPTER 11

LEVERAGE: TURNING STRATEGY INTO SUCCESS

Up to this point in *Sponsorship Strategy*, I have discussed structuring strategy to achieve the best sponsorship results. However, the most famous martial strategist, Sun Tzu, once said, "strategy without tactics is the slowest route to victory."[90] At some point, the sponsorship relationship moves from strategy into action. This process is called "leverage."

Leverage includes any activity that benefits the sponsor. These activities can include a product display at a sponsored event, social media using content from the sponsored property, or a public relations campaign featuring the benefits conferred on fans by the sponsorship.

Some people use the word "activation" to describe the same activities as leverage. Over time, there has been a trend in the industry to narrow the term "activation" to mean event displays. For clarity, I will use the broader term leverage.

I wanted to address leverage for a simple reason. As Sun Tzu implied in his quote, without great execution, the strategies described in *Sponsorship Strategy* will have little practical impact. In this chapter, I will explore the considerations that make for effective leverage activities, including the need for strategy integration and the importance of a close working relationship with properties for implementation.

The Importance of Integrated Marketing

To this point, I have written about sponsorship as if it were a discrete marketing tactic. It is. However, when a sponsorship is leveraged, it combines many different marketing tactics. Sponsors generally rely on channels including social media, public relations, hospitality, on-site experiential, and internal corporate communications.[91] For sponsorship to really work, it takes all these channels and more.

This chapter is not intended to be a primer in public relations, social media, or experiential marketing. Cutting-edge ideas should be left for the experts in those disciplines. However, if not properly integrated and executed into a single plan, the sponsorship impact is muted. Five tactics are like five fingers. An open hand has a fraction of the impact as a closed fist.

An integrated leverage plan must have the following elements:

A COMMON GOAL

All integrated activities should serve the sponsorship's common goal. This goal can be any of the objectives referenced in this book: increasing brand awareness, enhancing brand image, or improving sales. But for any goal, you should be able to draw a straight line between the facet of the integrated leverage plan (like PR) and the objective that you want sponsorship to achieve.

AUDIENCE FOCUSED

Not all audiences are created equal. A family-oriented event should have a different plan than an EDM concert.

Many times, leverage planning begins in the conference room of the brand's advertising agency of record (AOR) or the sponsorship manager's office. Unfortunately, its genesis is often a function of budget, existing personnel resources, or bias towards a particular marketing strategy. However, this process ought to be more strategic.

Billions of dollars are spent annually on rights fees. Strategically, these spends are sound. Rights fees buy brands the right the engage in positive image transfer with the property's audience. However, when it comes time to start making this transfer possible, many brands drop the ball with insufficient or poorly conceived leverage. A more strategic approach will ultimately boost the sponsor's impact.

Applying the learnings from previous chapters, an audience-focused integrated leverage plan will do the following:

- Underscore audience congruence or fit. It should organically support the proposition that it is natural for this brand to be associated with this event.
- Carefully balance the commercial goals of the sponsor

against the non-commercial atmosphere of the event. It should not appear like the reason you are there is to sell stuff.

- Be authentic and sincere. The brand wants to support an event for the benefit of its shared target audience. Make sure this message is loud and clear.
- Promote involvement in the event. Involvement increases receptivity to the brand's message. Immerse the audience in what the event is all about.

This leverage planning process begins by understanding what the audience wants – in general and from this particular sponsored event.

The process begins with the demographic and psychographic profile of the audience. The same data that made the sponsorship partnership happen can be a treasure trove of guidance about what types of activations will resonate with an audience. Audience personality and lifestyle data will provide clues about favorite activities, TV shows, books, sports, or how they like to spend their family time.

Sometimes the best ideas for leverage activities are intuitive. A sponsorship and experiential marketing team knows what will resonate based on experience with the same or similar audience. Experience is often the best teacher.

Other times, this process may not yield useful insights, so it is best to reach out and ask the audience. This may occur when a new sponsor, potentially one unfamiliar with a property, is not quite sure. In these circumstances, I'm reminded of the pre-internet days of gathering driving directions to reach a destination. Rather than circling in unknown territory while slowly running out of fuel, one passenger would turn to the driver and shout, "Will you just stop and ask for directions?!" In the case of activation planning, the same rules would apply: stop and ask your audience.

Pre-event, event, or post-event property surveys provide good information. New sponsors can either ask the property to administer such surveys or ask veteran co-sponsors of the event for this information. Similarly, this may be an opportunity for the brand to do its own audience survey to answer this question.

CONSISTENT MESSAGING

One of the hardest aspects of an effective integrated leverage plan is maintaining consistent messaging across marketing channels. The strength of integration lies in the seamless nature of it. The consumer is presented with a united front of messaging. This means that if a customer encounters the sponsorship on social, it will have the same tone and feel as what they see in a product display on site.

LEVERAGES THE BEST OF EACH OF YOUR MARKETING CHANNELS

Some leverage plans rely on established marketing channels without much strategic thought. A company may simply be familiar with these channels or they may be controlled by the sponsorship manager. However, careful consideration should be given to using the best channels for a target audience. Social media engagement may be good for one audience but not for another. Television may be less relevant to some audiences than others. Combine channels that work best for the sponsorship.

ENOUGH RESOURCES TO GET THE JOB DONE

When budgets allow, the best sponsorships represent integrated marketing at its finest. Brands frequently ask me to recommend an ideal ratio for their promotional spend. That is the ratio of rights fee to leverage and activation spending. This certainly varies from industry to industry and even brand to brand. Industries like consumer-packaged goods spend more on activation than the healthcare industry. However, in a recent survey,[92] spending ratios still maintain some robustness. Only 19% of sponsors surveyed said they spend less than 1:1 on their sponsorships; 24% reported spending 4:1.

I usually recommend the sponsors spend the least amount to attain their objectives and the most programming their internal staff and agency support can comfortably manage. If I were to quantify this amount, I would advise a 1:1 ratio at a minimum.

The Working Role of the Property

The property can and should exhibit leadership in leverage activities by setting the stage for successful programs and protecting them. This leadership can begin with several process issues, but it should move into more substantive areas.

For example, one sponsorship expert[93] recommends that the property provide three process items at the outset of the relationship:

- User-friendly guidelines
- A clear, efficient, dependable approval process
- Dedicated staff charged with operating and improving the process as it runs

Certainly, these resources will smooth out the rough edges of any new sponsorship relationship. However, the property should exercise more leadership in setting the tone for its sponsors' activation activities.

I understand that this is a delicate balancing act. You are a property's chief revenue officer, and you are still dancing in your office every day because you have signed a million dollars' worth of new sponsors. The last thing you want to do is insult your new brand partner's sponsorship team with unsolicited advice about how they should do their jobs. I have experienced that feeling from both sides.

However, leadership can take many forms. For those who wish to take a more delicate approach, do not advise what to do in the future. Instead, simply provide information about what has happened in the past. Effective strategies in this regard include the following:

- Case studies about successful activation activities by the property's existing or past sponsors

- Anecdotes about past activation failures, including the reasons for failure and countermeasures to prevent it
- Insights about the audience and trends regarding their preferences and behaviors
- Contact information of co-sponsors who have agreed to provide the new sponsor with insights about how to succeed in the property's environment.

If a property exercises proactive leadership around its sponsor's activation programs, everyone will benefit. The property can offer a robust and enjoyable attendee experience; the sponsor can enjoy greater benefit from its sponsorship; and the audience will receive greater value and enjoyment from the event. A classic win-win-win.

Creating Off-Site Resonance

If a sponsorship can be leveraged on-site, there is no reason that same sponsorship cannot resonate off-site. As marketers, we live in a miraculous time. For little or no cost, we can communicate globally with a key stroke. We have never had the opportunity to reach more people. This puts a premium on great storytelling through social media, digital marketing, and a variety of electronic media.

Because we can tell global stories, why do so many in sponsorship continue to view sponsored relationships through a narrow, geographic lens? An event sponsorship is often envisioned as anything that fits within the four corners of the event property. Or it may be the county, city, or town where the event is located. A larger DMA may be considered for media purposes. But what we really need to consider is how to make image transfer work on a much broader scale.

If image transfer can work on-site, we must consider how it could work on a wider basis. Today, we can make a sponsorship event in Lincoln, Nebraska resonate in Portland, Oregon. The power of photo, video, and storytelling enables virtual experiences that resonate with audiences well beyond the site of a sponsorship.

Using the Tools of Off-Site Impact

Let's consider a not-so-hypothetical. A well-known national bank sponsors a statewide youth soccer association. The bank wishes to demonstrate a commitment to its community, with the hope that it will drive traffic to retail banking locations throughout the state. In this case, one might consider the goals of the sponsorship to be limited to the soccer pitches of that state.

However, this relationship is certain to generate stories and imagery that convey support of youth development, gender equality, or family values that transcend the state's youth soccer association. Many times, the impact of this localized activity will not make it to the national offices of the bank's marketing staff. However, there are nuggets of awesomeness sitting in someone's Dropbox folder or on their hard drive.

Every great sponsorship story deserves to be leveraged far and wide. Image transfer that works locally will surely work more broadly if the same cultural underpinnings apply. But a sponsorship in one country may not translate well in another because of cultural differences.

Great stories have no boundaries. (Just be sure you have the contractual rights to tell that story beyond the physical site of the sponsorship and in accordance with the timeframe agreed by the brand and the property.) The following tools have never made it easier to carry great stories beyond an event site.

SOCIAL MEDIA

A Twitter post, Facebook Live event, or an Instagram story provide the best opportunity to make a sponsorship resonate. Compelling content will carry the image of the sponsor through the great story told on these channels.

PUBLIC RELATIONS / MEDIA RELATIONS

Generally, public and media relations aim at endemic media or regionalized media outlets. For this form of media, local outlets like to carry local stories, and national outlets rarely cover stories that do not have nationwide interest. However, sponsors can repost and further amplify media exposure through its own social media channels. For example, a local reporter's enthusiastic reaction to an event in Des Moines will play will in Albuquerque if carried there by a YouTube repost.

CORPORATE SOCIAL RESPONSIBILITY

It is more prevalent to have a charity or cause integrated into a sponsorship. Depending on the type of social responsibly program, it is possible, even likely, that the cause will be popular beyond the sponsorship locale. In all these cases, it takes hard work to keep great stories alive. However, if a story does manage to go viral, its resonance beyond the sponsored event looks like a masterstroke of sponsorship strategy.

The Benefits of Reaching Isolated, Avid Fans

Off-site resonance can be particularly impactful in certain circumstances. Specifically, avid fans of a property, living remotely, have greater affinity for the property's sponsors than avid fans living nearby.[94] Why? Because isolated avid fans crave connection to their favorite team, league, or athlete. A sponsor can serve as a valuable connection.

This leverage strategy enables practitioners to conserve budget resources while increasing sponsorship efficacy. Research has shown that exposure to a *single* sponsor advertisement among an avid and isolated audience produces comparable performance outcomes to a local audience that received *multiple* ad exposures.[95]

For the practitioner, practical strategies of off-site resonance could include several approaches. First, social media geo-targeting provides opportunities to reach an audience distant from a property. One of my sons adores Liverpool FC, but lives thousands of miles from his favorite English football club. There are numerous ways for the club's sponsors to speak to my son via social and digital media.

Second, watch parties for avid fans have been around for a long time. Think of the bars that host watch parties for out-of-city NFL fan clubs. Boosting this strategy with 21st century technology facilitates a connection between isolated avid fans and the property. Nothing connects people together more strongly than a bunch of ex-pats rooting for a far-off favorite team.

CHAPTER 12

VALIDATING STRATEGY THROUGH MEASUREMENT

The elephant in the room of every sponsorship discussion is measurement. It tends to be a sore point with CFOs because marketing departments do not live and die by measurement the same way they do. Marketers understand the need for it, but do not validate this need by allocating enough budget support for measurement. However, the industry cannot ignore this priority. As budgets get tighter and tighter, measurement is needed to validate the success (or failure) of great sponsorships.

Should We Do It?

Over the past decade, surveys of sponsorship managers report the same attitudes. Sponsorship managers want to measure the effectiveness of sponsorship and view it as important. However, when it comes time to measure, their actions often fall short of their intentions.

Only 37% of sponsorship managers report having a standardized process for sponsorship measurement.[96] When rubber hits the road, on average, sponsorship managers only allocate 5% or less (relative to the sponsorship fee) of their budget to measurement.

I do not believe there is any argument against measurement. Like any other business enterprise, measuring key performance indicators is the hallmark of success. However, I raise the following issues as a call to action to align good intention with results.

What Should We Do?

OVERALL STRATEGY AND OBJECTIVES

As the author Jim Collins said in his best-selling business book, *Good to Great*, you should always begin with the end in mind. You should have a clear sense of your sponsorship's strategic goals before you even begin negotiations.

If your objective is to increase brand awareness, you should have determined how to measure it. If your objective is to increase sales, you may have indicated by how much. In any event, measurement must be used to assess pre-defined sponsorship strategy and objectives.

Identifying strategy and objectives at the outset of a sponsorship enables all parties to understand the cost and effectiveness of the relationship. It also provides the opportunity to course-correct during the sponsorship term. If strategic elements are not being achieved, and you are aware of this issue early enough, the sponsor or property can make valuable adjustments to get back on track, thus ensuring success by the end of the term.

BASELINE EXPOSURE AND HEALTH

I have been both on the receiving and giving ends of many sponsorship measurement reports. Organizations use a variety of performance indicators, but in general, these are commonly considered baseline data points:

- Media impressions
- Social media engagement
- Attendance figures
- Television viewership

One school of thought rejects all these measures because they do not capture what is really important to a sponsor. I would agree that these measures are not the be-all, end-all. However, they are good indicators of baseline exposure and sponsorship health. There are several reasons for this.

First, they predict the requisite amount of work needed to make a sponsorship successful. Did the brand or property's PR team try to maximize impact? What was the relative quantum of social media? And was there enough consumer engagement? These metrics operate like the gauges in most automobiles. They will not tell you if you arrived at the destination, but they will indicate if the car is in good working order and running.

Second, they reveal the relative health of the sponsorship,

especially when compared over time. At the outset of a relationship, the brand has analyzed the audience. Just like any business, the brand wants that audience to grow. It is a sign of trouble when indicators for the event are weakening. It may not be time to pull the plug, but it may be time to ask questions.

RETURN ON OBJECTIVES

Return on objectives (ROO) measures describe the middle funnel goals a brand may have for the sponsorship. Things like brand awareness and preference as well as affinity. According to a recent survey by the Association of National Advertisers (ANA) and the Marketing Accountability Standards Board (MASB),[97] many brands rely on the following ROO measures:

- Awareness of brand
- Awareness of company/brand sponsorship
- Attitudes toward brand
- Amount of total media exposure
- Amount of social media exposure
- Brand preference
- Amount of TV exposure
- Entertainment of key customers / prospects
- Sentiment of social media exposure

If the superpower of sponsorship is image transfer, these measures may evaluate the impact of the sponsorship more directly than financial measures, which I define below. If tracked over time, a sponsorship manager can see direct evidence that the sponsorship is changing the hearts and minds of consumers. It is relatively safe to assume that a consumer who grows fonder of a brand will form a commercial relationship with that brand.

RETURN ON INVESTMENT

Return on investment (ROI) measures describe the financial return from a sponsorship. According to the ANA/MASB,[98] ROI measures include:

- Total sponsorship investment financial return
- Total media exposure financial return
- Product or service sales
- Social media exposure financial return
- TV exposure financial return
- Sponsorship-related promotions financial return
- Lower customer acquisition cost

These measures obviously provide some insights into the ROI value of a sponsorship. For example, if the sponsorship leads to media exposure, one could surmise there would be financial return in terms of sales. However, without other data, that would only be an assumption.

Also, these measures place a premium on a brand's knowledge of its sales pipeline. For instance, understanding the relationship between seeing a media clip and buying a product. It may be that for every 10,000 impressions, a brand enjoys $1,200 in revenue.

INVOLVE THE PROPERTY IN THE PROCESS

Great properties understand that, in the sponsorship arena, they must sing for their supper. This means that, on a regular basis, properties report to their sponsors on the results of the sponsorship relationship. This seems to be a good idea. However, it is more than that. Most brands reported that they consider it "important" or "extremely important" for the property to participate in measurement.[99]

In this same ANA/MASB survey, the top four measurement areas that properties need to provide are the following:

- Audience research on sponsor recognition and recall
- Audience research on attitudes about sponsors
- Audience research on behavior towards sponsors
- Audience demographics

In this area, I note a couple of recommendations. First, if measurement is important to a brand, consider addressing it in the sponsorship agreement, as noted in my discussion earlier on strategic contract terms. A failure to address this issue early in the relationship may prevent the sponsor from the opportunity to measure.

Second, if the brand intends on doing its own research into the property's audience, the brand should consider securing on-site or online access to them. Again, this is a term important enough to merit discussion when the agreement is negotiated.

What Should the Industry Do?

While sponsorship managers have traditionally been conflicted about measurement, the trends in business and the economy lead to one conclusion. Every marketing platform will be put under a microscope to determine return-on-investment and/or return-on-objectives. The Great Recession (2008-2010) increased demands to measure sponsorships. Without a doubt, in the years ahead, this direction will become even more important in sponsorship management.

In my opinion, the sponsorship industry has begun selecting the most impactful sponsorship measures. In another recent survey,[100] sponsors ranked the value of metrics in the following order:

1. Attitude towards the brand
2. Amount of positive social media activity
3. Awareness of products services or brand
4. Awareness of company's or brand's sponsorship
5. Product or service sales
6. Response to customer, prospect entertainment
7. Response to sponsorship related promotions or content
8. Amount of media exposure generated
9. TV logo exposure
10. Lead generation

Like their thoughts about objectives, sponsors from this survey valued cognitive and affective measures of sponsorship. However, all these measures are relevant to sponsorship effectiveness. The industry should commit to a "measurement game plan" for every partnership. I recommend selecting those measures from the preceding list that best fit a particular sponsorship and zealously adhere to those measures for evaluation sponsorship impact. If sponsorships are no longer evaluated by gut feel or anecdotal evidence, it fuels the inherent power they have as a marketing tool.

CHAPTER 13

RETHINKING THE SPONSOR SUMMIT TOOL

Everyone in the sponsorship industry has attended a sponsor summit. Most of these events are pretty much the same: a half-day or whole-day affair, generally requiring participants to fly in from across the country (or the world). There may or may not be a social event, like a dinner or cocktail reception.

During the business portion of the summit, participants passively sit and listen to presentations from the property's staff. The presentations contain information that could have been transmitted by email, but the property's staff feels they need to put on a show. There may be a short speech from the property's chief or senior executive, who then promptly leave the summit, giving the inadvertent impression that the summit was not worth their time.

Sound familiar?

In-person communication is a powerful part of the sponsorship relationship. It is also a contributor to great sponsorship strategy. However, rather than thinking about it as a check-the-box activity, the property should think of it as a chance to make it the "strategy capstone of value creation." A once-a-year opportunity to offer impactful and memorable value for the sponsor.

Several best practices have been identified in this area.[101] The common denominator of all best practices is careful planning and thoughtful attention to content. Ask, "when the sponsor goes home, what will he or she have learned and felt was valuable for their investment of time?" Here are my recommendations on how to spice up this otherwise bland experience.

STATE OF THE PROPERTY PRESENTATION

Many of you have heard State of the Property speeches before. (Cue the *Battle Hymn of the Republic*). Without radically departing from the current format, I have a few ideas for how to make these presentations more impactful for sponsors.

First, provide verifiable and accessible data about the performance of the property. If data is cited in the presentation, make the presentation or the data available after the speech.

Second, provide insights that were likely unknown to sponsors. In some cases, the sponsors may have more data than the property. Here, you might even consider giving the sponsor time to present its data. However, the property is in a unique position to provide insights about what that data means. Help interpret good (and bad) news for sponsors with the property's unique insights. In terms of any bad news, the property should not be naïve enough to try to hide it. Any problems will be exposed eventually. Instead, the property should be able to explain any negative outcomes because it may be the only chance to save the sponsorship long-term.

Third, detail the property's business strategy for the coming year. Not a summary of a strategy or a wish list without budget approval from the CFO. Give participants a real sense of where the property is going strategically.

Remember: The sponsorship manager must return to his or her office and report on the prospects of the property. How do you want him or her to report on this event and the brand's investment in the sponsorship?

CROSS-POLLINATION OF IDEAS

Some properties give the podium to the sponsor to provide a (too) long presentation of their complete sponsorship program. Instead, structure opportunities for sponsors to offer a few best practices, results from their most innovative programs, and reflections on working in the property's environment. Sure, the sponsors want to brag a little about their accomplishments. However, the purpose here is to strengthen every co-sponsor's program by providing real-world ideation about what works best for each sponsor. A workshop environment works best for cross-pollination.

INTRODUCTIONS / ICE BREAKERS

In a recent summit, I wanted to meet as many co-sponsors as possible. But I walked out knowing only half the sponsors.

The few conversations I did have with new acquaintances ended up being valuable for me and our client. What if I had met *everyone* in attendance?

"Speed introductions" (like speed dating, only more professional!) have become a frequently maligned tool of sponsor meetings. However, I have found few other activities that are as impactful in facilitating mass introductions. Do you really get more out of the alternative: people standing up and announcing their name, title, and company affiliation?

Consideration should also be given to ice-breaker exercises. Like the tool used in meeting facilitation, ice breakers can be used in groups of five to fifteen to facilitate low pressure and enjoyable introductions.

When used effectively, these techniques are valuable to connect a name with a face. They open the door to real conversations about best practices and value creation, which benefit both properties and brands.

RECOGNITION / ACHIEVEMENT AWARDS

Everyone likes to be recognized for special achievement. This area is always a bit tricky in the sponsor environment because every sponsor likes to feel appreciated for its contribution. And, the property finds itself in the position of a parent who does not want one child to feel more loved than another.

Nevertheless, recognition serves a valuable purpose. It highlights appreciation for a sponsor and its investment.

However, rather than singling out a single sponsor with an award, why not think of recognizing sponsors with unique categories that are important. For instance, the Most Innovative Sponsorship Tactic of the Year, the Winning under Pressure Award, or the Rookie of the Year award. Be creative and prolific in your praise.

GUEST SPEAKER

If one of your summit goals involves an educational component, I suggest serving up informative content. Properties should consider guest speakers that can address new or important issues relevant to the sponsorship industry. Prominent expert guest speakers add an impactful dimension to a sponsorship summit. And some speakers are so alluring, your sponsor's CEO may decide to show up at the meeting.

Potential topics could include psychographics of Millennials and Gen Z, reaching diverse audiences through sponsorship, or leveraging technology in sponsorship. This type of content not only leaves a sponsorship manager with a clear sense of value from a property's summit, it establishes the property as a thought leader.

CHAPTER 14

STRATEGIC THOUGHTS

While many of my colleagues appreciate a well-executed campaign or an astounding viral moment on Twitter, I love a well-crafted strategy. Maybe this is one of the reasons I enjoy the sponsorship industry so much. The sponsorship strategies developed in this area are as varied as the brands and properties involved in it.

There are dozens of sports, both amateur and professional. Hundreds of types of humanities organizations or cause-based not-for-profits. With each brand and each property comes a new opportunity for a different strategy to help both parties find success in their commercial relationship.

In the course of *Sponsorship Strategy*, I discussed a variety of approaches that can help you amp up the power of your sponsorships. Many of these strategies have several overarching themes in common, and I wanted to close this book by summarizing these themes.

AUTHENTICITY

Whether it is sponsor fit or reasons for CSR integration, authenticity is important. It is vital for sponsors and properties to "be real" in their reasons for sponsorship relationships. Sponsorships can be successful because consumers let their guards down to partnerships, not commercial messages. They are more inclined to feel better about sponsors that support the events they love.

When sponsorships come about for the wrong reasons, they violate that trust. For this reason, sponsors should resist the urge to endorse an activity merely to keep their competitors out of the category. They should not sponsor the hot new property merely because it is the hot new property. They should not try to be something that they are not.

The mantra "to thine own self be true" applies as much in sponsorship as it does in Shakespearean literature.

COMMUNICATE, COMMUNICATE, COMMUNICATE

Many professionals are responsible for great sponsorships. However, the event activation professionals and their experiential agency are often lauded as the heroes of sponsorship. While I would never want to diminish the important role that this form of leverage plays in the sponsorship mix, my "heroes of sponsorship strategy" award go to the pros who work in public relations and social media departments.

Why?

Because the often-overlooked part of sponsorship strategy is explaining the "why" of the relationship. Even in the most authentic sponsorships, motivations may not be transparent. Therefore, many of the strategies articulated in the preceding pages involve communicating the fit of the sponsorship relationship – starting with the first press conference or the first press release. And, this reasoning should continue in communication thereafter, including social media tactics employed all the way through event time.

Just as a mentor of mine often reminded me, "you ain't done it unless people know about it."

THINK GLOBALLY, ACT LOCALLY

Just because an event is local, its impact can be felt around the world. The type of relationship, the emotions elicited from fans, the special moments created are not all tied to a local sponsorship venue.

The best sponsorships touch the human heart. They spark an emotional connection. These are all things that resonate far and wide. Accordingly, off-site resonance and other communications strategies should allow the sponsorship to transcend its event-based roots.

SPONSORSHIP AS LIFE

Marketers are fortunate. Some disciplines in business are cold and two-dimensional. However, marketing is about storytelling, pulling at heart strings and persuasion. At times though, it is not very measurable. But it can be emotionally satisfying when you see a client, or their clients, cry with joy about something you have created. If you are lucky, this will happen at some point in your career.

That is why it perplexes me that so many marketers take a "set it and forget it" approach to sponsorship. It is often treated like signage erected on a stadium wall. It is as if the sponsorship were some static representation of a symbol meant to achieve an outcome only by its sheer presence.

In *Sponsorship Strategy*, I have outlined how to leverage the sponsorship relationship. Perhaps I have spent too much time on the leverage part and too little on the relationship part. Let me correct that now.

Sponsorships are based on relationships. It is the relationship that generates amazing results for brands and properties. Relationships work, in business and in life, because they generate and embody emotion.

It is the love for a child, the connection to a friend, the compassion for a stranger in need, or the loyalty to a business partner. These relationships generate emotions of all kinds: positive feelings of happiness, comfort, or nostalgia. Or negative feelings like disappointment, anger, or pain.

By viewing sponsorship the same way you look at personal relationships, you can use the lessons you've already learned to practice better sponsorship strategy.

Any spouse or significant other will tell you that the quality of their relationship is directly proportional to the effort put into it. It can be simple things like remembering birthdays or more complex issues like weathering a health crisis. Whether it is understanding the needs and wants of your spouse or significant other, becoming adept at problem solving, or being accommodating on the right occasions, the more you work, the stronger the relationship.

At the same time, when a relationship is neglected, parties grow distant from or antagonistic to one another. The relationship becomes a burden and is something to be avoided. Eventually, it dies on the vine.

The sponsorship relationship is the same. It requires investment at several levels. Personal investment to create bonds between brand and property employees. The investment of time to fully understand the property's audience, with all the nuances enveloped in that. Financial investment in a comprehensive leverage strategy to announce to the world the importance of the relationship. When all these things happen, happiness ensues in the forms of great ROI and ROO.

The opposite is true for neglected sponsorship relationships. They become a burden. They are unproductive emotionally and empirically.

It almost goes without saying that compatibility, at some level, is a pre-condition to a great relationship. At the beginning of a marriage, there are shared interests, common values, and a bit of physical attraction and spark. There was laughter and a host of activities enjoyed together.

If you met your spouse at a party, it was probably an event filled with other people who had many of the same interests. Perhaps you attended the same college, enjoyed the same music, or worked in the same industry. There was a commonality, and you felt like you fit in at the party.

The sponsorship relationship is the same. Brands fit their property partners, either in terms of category fit of personality fit. Common interests create natural pairings. Most importantly, the pairing must not only seem natural to the brand and property; it must be immediately apparent to the audience. Just like feeling out of place at a party or dating someone who isn't quite right, the audience knows when a brand and property just don't fit together.

ONWARD

Sponsorship has survived recessions, new marketing movements, and technology upheavals. This speaks to its intrinsic value. A relationship will always be important to the value creation equation. The value that a brand and property can create, resulting in consumer value, is a win-win-win that supports strong return on investment. What is not to like about that?

I hope that *Sponsorship Strategy* can help you maximize the value of this powerful marketing tool. For the brand that wants to increase awareness and sales, there is a sponsorship that fits you. For the property that wants to monetize its powerful brand, there is a partner who wants to join forces with you. And, for the sponsorship professional bringing parties together in happy matrimony, I wish you continued success. I will see you at the event!

Ken Ungar

ABOUT THE AUTHOR

KEN UNGAR is the president and founder of CHARGE, a sponsorship marketing agency that helps brands and properties unlock the power of sponsorship. Since its founding 2006, CHARGE has served clients including Honda, Acura, NASCAR, the Los Angeles Dodgers, NBA Players Association, American Motorcyclist Association, Sports Car Club of America, and over fifty professional athletes in the NFL, NASCAR, and IndyCar.

Ungar has worked as a marketer, league representative, event promoter, and business leader at the highest levels of professional sports. He is an attorney and has been a member of the American Marketing Association and the Sports Lawyers Association. In 2014, Ungar was certified as a player contract advisor by the NFL Players Association.

His experience in sports business, personal branding, media training, sponsorships, and endorsements as well as agents and legal issues led him to author "Ahead of the Game: What Every Athlete Needs to Know About Sports

Business." Ungar also teaches these important concepts to athletes and teams at sports business seminars across the country.

Ungar has worked with marquis brands on sports sponsorships and endorsements, including Bombardier Aerospace, Bridgestone-Firestone, Coca Cola, Disney, General Motors, Honda, Jim Beam, Microsoft, Nissan, Pepsi, Pioneer, Reebok, Tag-Heuer, Toyota, Sirius-XM Satellite Radio, and more.

Ungar's media interviews have been carried by numerous shows and outlets, including ABC News, Advertising Age, The Associated Press, Chicago Tribune, CNBC, CNN Money, ESPN, Forbes, Fox Business, Fox News, "Good Morning America," Los Angeles Times, Marketing Daily, The New York Times, Sports Business Journal, Sports Illustrated, USA Today, Washington Post, and "World News Tonight."

From 1997 through 2005, Ungar served as Chief of Staff of the Indianapolis Motor Speedway and Senior Vice President of INDYCAR.

Before entering sports, Ungar achieved success in other business arenas. He began his professional career as a practicing attorney where he directed legal matters and handled litigation for corporate clients. Ungar then moved to public service, where he served for four years as deputy chief of staff and executive assistant for government operations for Indiana Governor Evan Bayh.

Ungar is a graduate of Indiana University with a

bachelor's degree in political science and business administration. He went on to graduate from Columbia University with a law degree. He currently resides in Zionsville, Indiana, with his wife and two sons.

ENDNOTES

INTRODUCTION

1   Kissoudi, P. "Closing the Circle: Sponsorship and the Greek Olympic Games from Ancient Times to the Present Day," *The International Journal of the History of Sport, 22* no. 4 (2005): 618-638.

2   Gross, P. *Growing Brands Through Sponsorship: An Empirical Investigation of Brand Image Transfer in a Sponsorship Alliance.* Hanover, Germany, Springer, 2014.

3   Statista. Global Sponsorship Spending from 2007 to 2018. https://www.statista.com/statistics/196864/global-sponsorship-spending-since-2007/ (Accessed April 18, 2020).

4   Sport Dimensions. Why You Should Focus on Sponsorship Activation. https://www.sd.team/feed/why-we-do-it-sponsorship-activation (Accessed April 18, 2020).

CHAPTER 1

5   American Marketing Association. Definitions of Marketing. https://www.ama.org/the-definition-of-marketing/ (Accessed Oct. 4, 2019).

6   Smart Insights. The Big List of Today's Marketing Channels. https://www.

smartinsights.com/online-brand-strategy/multichannel-strategies/select-marketing-channels/ (Accessed Oct. 4, 2019).

7 MASB. Sponsorship. https://marketing-dictionary.org/s/sponsorship/ (Accessed Dec. 8, 2019).

8 Merriam-Webster. Sponsor. https://www.merriam-webster.com/dictionary/sponsor (Accessed Oct. 4, 2019).

9 MASB. Advertising. https://marketing-dictionary.org/a/advertising/ (Accessed Dec. 8, 2019).

10 Business Dictionary. Event Marketing. http://www.businessdictionary.com/definition/event-marketing.html (Accessed June 1, 2020).

11 MASB. Experiential Marketing. https://marketing-dictionary.org/e/experiential-marketing/ (Accessed Dec. 8, 2019).

12 Sports Business Journal's Sports Marketing Symposium, New York, NY. October 15, 2019.

13 ANA/MASB, Improving Sponsorship Accountability Metrics, July 2018.

CHAPTER 2

14 Bleacher Report. The Top 10 Fanbases in American Sports. https://bleacherreport.com/articles/1230923-top-10-fan-bases-in-american-sports (Accessed May 23, 2020).

15 Dosh, K. Measuring the Cost of being a Sports Fan. *Forbes*. https://www.forbes.com/sites/kristidosh/2018/09/30/measuring-the-cost-of-being-a-sports-fan/#44ec7ead5e54 (Accessed May 23, 2020).

16 Wroblewski, M.T. What are Examples of Demographics? *Small Business Chronicle*. https://smallbusiness.chron.com/examples-demographics-65678.html (Accessed Oct. 4, 2019).

17 Sharma, P.K. (2019). *Thinking Salesman*. Chennai: Thinking Press.

18 Senise, J. "Who Is Your Next Customer?". *Booz Allen Hamilton Inc,*

Strategy+Business. 28 September 2007. https://www.strategy-business. com/article/07313?_ref= (Accessed June 1, 2020).

19   MBA Skool Team. Behavioral Segmentation. https://www.mbaskool. com/business-concepts/marketing-and-strategy-terms/2542-behavioral-segmentation.html (Accessed January 9, 2020)

20   MBA Skool Team. Behavioral Segmentation. https://www.mbaskool. com/business-concepts/marketing-and-strategy-terms/2542-behavioral-segmentation.html (Accessed January 9, 2020)

CHAPTER 3

21   Ross, S., and Chen, Q. "Post Adoption Attitudes to Advertising on the Internet." *Journal of Advertising Research, 42* no. 5 (2002): 95-104.

22   Do, H. and Ko, E. and Woodside, A. "Tiger Woods, Nike, and I are (Not) Best Friends: How Brand's Sports Sponsorship in Social-Media Impacts Brand Consumer's Congruity and Relationship Quality." *International Journal of Advertising, 34* no. 4 (2015): pp. 658-677

23   IEG Sponsorship Report. Sponsor Survey Reveals Dissatisfaction with Property Partners. http://www.sponsorship.com/Report/2017/12/18/ Sponsor-Survey-Reveals-Dissatisfaction-With-Proper.aspx (Accessed Oct. 5, 2019).

CHAPTER 4

24   Grohs, R., & Reisinger, H. "Image transfer in sports sponsorships: an assessment of moderating effects." *International Journal of Sports Marketing and Sponsorship, 7* no. 1 (2005): 36-42.

25   Chien, P., Cornwell, T., & Pappu, R. "Sponsorship portfolio as a brand-image creation strategy." *Journal of Business Research, 64* no. 2(2011): 142-149.

26 Schimmelpfennig, C., & Hunt, J. "Fifty years of celebrity endorser research: Support for a comprehensive celebrity endorsement strategy framework." *Psychology & Marketing, 37* no. 3(2020): 488-505.

27 Schimmelpfennig, C., & Hunt, J. "Fifty years of celebrity endorser research: Support for a comprehensive celebrity endorsement strategy framework." *Psychology & Marketing, 37* no. 3(2020): 488-505.

28 Gwinner, K. "A model of image creation and image transfer in event sponsorship." *International Marketing Review, 14* no. 3(1997): 145-158.

29 Gwinner, K. "A model of image creation and image transfer in event sponsorship." *International Marketing Review, 14* no. 3(1997): 145-158.

30 Gwinner, K. "A model of image creation and image transfer in event sponsorship." *International Marketing Review, 14* no. 3(1997): 145-158.

31 Pracejus, John W. "Seven Psychological Mechanisms Through Which Sponsorship Can Influence Consumers." In *Sports Marketing and the Psychology of Marketing Communication*, 2004. (pp. 175-190).

32 Alonso-Dos-Santos, M., Vveinhardt, J., Calabuig-Moreno, F., Montoro-Rios, F., Involvement and Image Transfer in Sports Sponsorship, *Inzinerine Ekonomika-Engineering Economics, 27* no. 1(2016): 78-89.

33 Plewa, C., & Quester, P. "Sponsorship and CSR: is there a link? A conceptual framework." *International Journal of Sports Marketing and Sponsorship, 12,* no. 4(2011): 22-38.

34 Rowady, J. How to Turn a Non-Endemic Sponsor into a 'New Endemic' Sponsor. https://www.mediapost.com/publications/article/249124/how-to-turn-a-non-endemic-sponsor-into-a-new-ende.html (Accessed Oct. 6, 2019).

35 Interview with Rod Davis, January 24, 2020.

36 Speed, R., & Thompson, P. "Determinants of sports sponsorship response." *Journal of the Academy of Marketing Science, 28,* no. 2(2008): 226-238.

37   Vance, L., Raciti, M., & Lawley, M. "Beyond brand exposure: measuring the sponsorship halo effect." *Measuring Business Excellence, 20* no. 3(2016).

38   Speed, R., & Thompson, P. "Determinants of sports sponsorship response." *Journal of the Academy of Marketing Science, 28* no. 2 (2008): 226-238.

39   Meenaghan, T. "Ambush Marketing – A Threat to Corporate Sponsorship. MIT Sloan Management Review." 1996. https://sloanreview.mit. edu/article/ambush-marketing-a-threat-to-corporate-sponsorship/ (Accessed September 24, 2019).

40   Speed, R., & Thompson, P. "Determinants of sports sponsorship response." *Journal of the Academy of Marketing Science, 28* no. 2 (2008): 226-238.

41   Plewa, C., & Quester, P. "Sponsorship and CSR: is there a link? A conceptual framework." *International Journal of Sports Marketing and Sponsorship, 12,* no. 4(2011): 22-38.

42   Grohs, R., & Reisinger, H. "Image transfer in sports sponsorships: an assessment of moderating effects." *International Journal of Sports Marketing and Sponsorship, 7,* no. 1 (2005): 36-42.

43   Alonso-Dos-Santos, M., Vveinhardt, J., Calabuig-Moreno, F., Montoro-Rios, F. "Involvement and Image Transfer in Sports Sponsorship," *Inzinerine Ekonomika-Engineering Economics, 27,* no. 1(2016): 78-89.

44   Alonso-Dos-Santos, M., Vveinhardt, J., Calabuig-Moreno, F., Montoro-Rios, F. "Involvement and Image Transfer in Sports Sponsorship," *Inzinerine Ekonomika-Engineering Economics, 27,* no. 1(2016): 78-89.

45   Chien, P., Cornwell, T., & Pappu, R. "Sponsorship portfolio as a brand-image creation strategy." *Journal of Business Research, 64,* no. 2 (2011): 142-149.

46 Wiedmann, K., & Gross, P. "Image Transfer in a Sponsorship Alliance." *Thexis, 30* no. 1 (2013): 22-35.

47 Speed, R., & Thompson, P. "Determinants of sports sponsorship response." *Journal of the Academy of Marketing Science, 28* no. 2 (2008): 226-238.

48 GlobeNewswire. Churchill Downs and Ford Motor Company Partner for the Kentucky Derby. https://www.globenewswire.com/news-release/2020/03/09/1997197/0/en/Churchill-Downs-and-Ford-Motor-Company-Partner-for-the-Kentucky-Derby.html (Accessed April 20, 2020).

CHAPTER 6

49 Impressions. Market Watch B2C vs B2B. https://impressionsmagazine.com/build-your-business/trends/market-watch-b2c-vs-b2b/ (Accessed June 1, 2020).

50 The Balance Careers. The Difference Between B2B Sales and B2C Sales and How They Work. https://www.thebalancecareers.com/what-is-b2b-sales-2917368 (Accessed June 1, 2020).

51 Kotler, P. and Pfoertsch, W. B2B Brand Management, 117 (2006).

52 The Bizzabo Blog. 2020 Event Marketing Statistics, Trends, and Data. https://blog.bizzabo.com/event-marketing-statistics (Accessed June 1, 2020).

53 Clark, J., Lachowetz, T., Irwin, R., & Schimmel, K. "Business-to-Business Relationships and Sport: Using Sponsorship as a Critical Sales Event." *International Journal of Sports Marketing and Sponsorship, 5* no. 2(2003): 38-53.

54 PPAI. 2018 Promotional Products Fact Sheet. http://www.promotionalproductswork.org/media/1217/law_2018propro-factsheet.pdf (Accessed June 1, 2020).

CHAPTER 7

55   Chen, J. "Corporate Social Responsibility," Investopia.com, https://www.investopedia.com/terms/c/corp-social-responsibility.asp (Accessed Sept. 22, 2019).

56   2017 Cone Communications Study. http://www.conecomm.com/research-blog/2017-csr-study (Accessed Sept. 22, 2019).

57   Digital Marketing Institute. 16 Brands doing Corporate Social Responsibility Successfully. https://digitalmarketinginstitute.com/en-us/blog/corporate-16-brands-doing-corporate-social-responsibility-successfully (Accessed Jan. 12, 2020).

58   The 2020 World's Most Ethical Companies Honoree List. https://www.worldsmostethicalcompanies.com/honorees/?fwp_country=united-states (Accessed June 1, 2020).

59   IEG Sponsorship Report. Survey Finds Sponsors Looking for Slightly Different Benefits and Services from Properties. https://www.sponsorship.com/iegsr/2014/03/31/Survey-Finds-Sponsors-Looking-For-Slightly-Differe.aspx (Accessed April 20, 2020).

60   Varadarajan, P.R. and Menon, A. "A coalignment of marketing strategy and corporate philanthropy," *Journal of Marketing, 52* no. 3 (1988): pp. 58-74.

61   Sung, M., & Lee, W. "What makes an effective CSR program? An analysis of the constructs of a cause-related participant sport sponsorship event." *International Journal of Sports Marketing and Sponsorship, 17* no. 1 (2016): 56-77.

62   Plewa, C., & Quester, P. "Sponsorship and CSR: is there a link? A conceptual framework." *International Journal of Sports Marketing and Sponsorship, 12,* no. 4(2011): 22-38.

63   Vance, L., Raciti, M., & Lawley, M. "Beyond brand exposure: measuring the